THE VODKA
COOKBOOK

THE VODKA COOKBOOK

JOHN ROSE

PHOTOGRAPHY BY SIMON WHEELER

KYLE CATHIE LTD

FOREWORD

Long before any cocktail ever splashed across my gums, I recall Smirnoff as the first spirits brand I recognised by name. After all, the two most important men of my formative years kept bottles of Smirnoff in their liquor cabinets – Dad and James Bond. And there is little doubt it was the first vodka I ever sipped. So I was tickled to learn that the Smirnoff Company wanted to play a part in bringing The Vodka Cookbook into the world. And out of courtesy and curiosity (and because my publisher told me to) I decided to sneak a peek behind the curtain of the best-selling vodka in the galaxy.

It's a remarkable story, really.

The distillery founded in 1864 by Piotr Arseneevich Smirnov became the most celebrated in Russia – eventually elevated to Purveyor to the Imperial Court for its quality. And Smirnov was showered with honours and fame from Paris to Philadelphia. Then, as in most every Russian tale, events turned tragic on an epic scale. Piotr died. Government monopolisation forced the Smirnov distillery out of the vodka business. And finally, the Bolshevik revolution closed its doors permanently. Piotr's son, Vladimir, who once socialised with the literary and theatrical elite of the day – Gorky, Chekhov, Stanislavski – was indicted as an 'enemy of the people'. He joined the anti-Bolshevik White Army and was assigned to escort refugees to safety. But Bolshevik soldiers ambushed his train and Vladimir was captured and sentenced to death. Tortured with daily threats of execution, Vladimir must have resigned himself to his fate when Fortune finally smiled upon him. The White Army overtook the prison where he was held and Vladimir was liberated. But, still a marked man, he was forced to flee Russia with little more than the clothes on his back... and a legacy of vodka-making expertise. Vladimir eventually made his way to France where he fell in love with a former chorus girl and Russian émigrée, Tatiana. Smirnov became 'Smirnoff'. And, against all odds, Vladimir revived the family business at a distillery outside Paris by 1933.

(I wonder who will play Vladimir in the movie?)

Obviously the saga didn't end there. Fortuitously, the revival of the Smirnoff brand in France coincided with the repeal of Prohibition in the United States. However Smirnoff languished in the US for many years until the popularity of the Bloody Mary, Screwdriver, Vodka Martini and Moscow Mule – made famous by clever Smirnoff celebrity endorsements – catapulted Smirnoff into the forefront of the newly emerging cocktail culture it helped to create.

I'm not prone to gush. But the more I learn about The Smirnoff Company, the more I admire their vodkas. Despite the enormous scale of their operation (they are now owned by spirits giant Diageo), they remain dedicated to the Smirnov legacy, committed to using only the finest ingredients and obsessive about purity to the point of employing one of the industry's most elaborate charcoal filtration processes. And they know a good cookbook when they see one. All of which has renewed my respect for a brand I associate with decades of good cheer. I'm delighted they came along for the ride.

INTRODUCTION

Living and working in Moscow, I have discovered that vodka plays as important a role in Russia as wine does in France or Italy. One day it occurred to me that, although vodka is arguably the world's most popular spirit, I have seldom seen it used in cooking. (And here I was in the vodka centre of the universe!) This was particularly striking because in Russia vodka and food are inseparable. Most Russians dine and entertain almost exclusively at home where the table is always set with *zafuski* (appetisers), including pelmeni, caviar and blini, black bread and the omnipresent bottle of vodka. Yet actually *cooking* with vodka is quite uncommon.

Out of curiosity, I began collecting the few decent vodka recipes I could find and went to work creating my own. Along the way, I started infusing vodka with a variety of flavourings and then incorporating it into my dishes. Through trial and error, and more than my share of culinary catastrophes, I learned what I could about the effects of vodka on other ingredients. And, after a few years of cooking in the evenings and at weekends, I found I had developed a respectable collection of recipes with one thing in common – vodka. Many of them are in the pages that follow. (The rest will eventually make it to my website: www.vodkacookbook.com)

This book is an eclectic collection of foods influenced by many different cuisines – from French to Italian, Mexican to Russian. In some recipes the vodka is used simply to perk up a classic dish. But in most cases the vodka is integral to the result and creates a unique and flavourful meal.

In addition to dinners and desserts, you will discover how to create Food Flights – soup-like shooters that blur the line between drinks and foods. You will also learn how to make flavoured vodka infusions and use them to whip up your own unique dishes and drinks. This book also includes some cool cocktail concoctions. But I'm betting you will soon be moving your vodka out of the liquor cabinet and into the kitchen cabinet.

Of course, there is something more to these recipes than just the way the food tastes. You tell someone there is vodka in their dinner or dessert and their eyes widen; their lips curl into a smile. An ordinary meal becomes an extraordinary event. And that's before a single forkful. I have witnessed this almost-magical effect many times since I began working on this book. And I'm guessing it is one reason why you now hold it in your hands.

'Candy is dandy, but liquor is quicker,' wrote American humourist Ogden Nash. 'Why can't we have our cake and drink it too?' say I.

Cheers!

JOHN ROSE
MOSCOW, RUSSIA

HOW TO USE THIS BOOK

Even one of these recipes would be enough to spice up any meal and add spirit (pun intended) to any gathering. Match two or more of these dishes and you will create a dining experience your friends and family may not soon forget – especially if you add chilled glasses of your favourite vodka (launched with a few of your favourite toasts), and finally send them on their way with some home-made vodka infusions (but without their car keys).

Just as you should always cook with the best wines, be sure to use premium vodka in all these recipes. I generally recommend Russian vodka for authenticity – or those made by Smirnoff which, though not produced in Russia, has a legitimate Russian pedigree and a high quality to which I can attest. However, there are many fine vodkas produced in other countries. So I will leave the selection up to you.

Some of these recipes take a bit of planning; insomuch as they require the advance preparation of certain items such as those in the Vodka Pantry chapter. You will also need a few vodka infusions – many of which require days or weeks of waiting (though mere minutes of preparation). But it will be worth the extra effort to take credit for some truly unique and flavourful dishes. In some cases you may substitute ready-made ingredients or commercially flavoured vodkas, if time does not allow you to prepare them yourself. (I won't tell.) Be aware, though, that certain infusions prescribed here may significantly differ from the shop-bought brands. I have indicated where alternative ingredients may be used whenever practical.

Most important, none of these recipes is beyond the capability of the average cook. In fact, I have added extra description and salted (and peppered) the book with helpful tips to aid beginners. Trust me. If I can cook it, so can you.

I also believe that cooking is a blend of art and science that benefits most from experimentation. Only you know what you like. If you prefer spicy foods, feel free to add extra seasoning or ingredients to achieve the desired result. Don't like garlic? Leave it out. And there is no need to follow these recipes religiously. Though I have had to become more disciplined during the preparation of this book, I rarely measure ingredients when I'm cooking for myself (other than perhaps when baking – which is as much chemistry as cooking). As long as you more or less maintain the balance of liquid to dry ingredients and monitor your heat, you shouldn't go too far astray. There is no need to turn these recipes into lab experiments – I mean... if you can't have fun with a vodka cookbook, you may need to seek professional help.

The recipes have been more or less arranged by purpose and main ingredient with many side dishes and sauces presented together with the entrée to provide a complete meal. But they're your taste buds. So feel free to mix and match recipes to create your own combinations.

What about all the alcohol? Obviously you should not serve vodka to children or others who do not or should not consume alcohol. However, in most of these recipes, much of the alcohol is eliminated during the cooking process – after having done the job of concentrating or intensifying certain flavours. (More on this in the next section.) In the end, you must use your own discretion when preparing and serving these dishes. And, of course, I recommend that when we do consume alcohol – in all its forms – we do so responsibly.

One more thing... just as we should drink alcohol in moderation, I believe the best way to stay healthy is not by denying ourselves rich or flavourful foods, but by consuming them less often and in reasonable quantities. So you won't find calorie counts next to any of these dishes. You also won't find fat or carbohydrate contents (vodka has neither, by the way). I would rather drink and eat in moderation (as well as spend a few extra hours at my fitness club) than forego any of my favourite foods. I hope you agree.

MENUS

While just one of the recipes in this book will add novelty to any meal, it can be more fun to present several vodka dishes – providing a unique theme to a special gathering. And if you co-ordinate your menu carefully, it doesn't have to be a chore to cook a full-course vodka dinner.

The secret to serving several courses is to select as many recipes that can be prepared in advance as possible. That way you can keep your sanity and spend more time with your guests.

To get you started, here are a few sample menu combinations. I am certain many more will become obvious once you get inspired. And nothing inspires quite like vodka.

WHAT'S FOR BRUNCH?

Champagnsky Koktail, see page 155
Russian Toast with Bananas Flambé and
    Raspberry-lime Vodka Sauce, see page 20
Vodka Fruit Flight, see page 45
Hot White Russian, see page 153

WHAT'S FOR DINNER?

Vodka-steamed Prawn Cocktail, see page 37
Stoned Crab Cakes with Orange Vodka
    Pineapple Salsa, see page 89
Habeñero-encrusted Tuna with Lemon Vodka
    and Thyme Dressing, see page 95
Lemon/Lime Vodka Granita, see page 114

HAVING A PARTY?

An assortment of Food Flights, beginning on
    page 38
Over-heated Tomatoes (with fresh buffalo
    mozzarella and drizzled with olive oil), see
    page 33
Distilled Bruschetta, see page 29

A glass for the vodka,
for the beer a mug,
and for the table, cheerful company
Popular Russian toast

VODKA BASICS

Where and when it was first invented is the subject of some debate. But without question, no country is more closely identified with vodka than Russia. Russian historians (naturally) take credit for the birth of vodka and claim it was first distilled in their country in the fifteenth century. The original product was crude and impure. But it must have done the trick because, six centuries later, vodka is more popular than ever. So break out a cold bottle of your favourite vodka and follow along as we cover a few vodka basics.

DRINKING

Vodka has become the world's most popular spirit because it is an ideal, neutral base for mixed drinks – and, as you'll soon discover, for dozens of foods. Nevertheless, I encourage you also to learn to appreciate it in its purest form.

Vodka should always be served chilled. But avoid pouring it over ice at all cost (though I make an exception for infused vodkas and cocktails). Alcohol is nature's antifreeze and will melt the ice immediately – turning your premium vodka into a watery shadow of its former self.

Fine-quality vodka with a tight seal can be kept in your freezer almost indefinitely without fear of it freezing. Alternatively, you can rinse glasses in cold water and store them in your freezer (upside down so that ice doesn't collect inside) so you are always at the ready. Even tepid vodka will quickly chill to an acceptable temperature in a frozen glass. I have also experimented with special ice trays that freeze water into the shape of shot glasses. Very cool... umm... cold.

Vodka, by definition, is a spirit without distinctive character, aroma, taste, or colour. However, when compared side-by-side, you will discover that there are distinct differences - based on ingredients, distillation and filtration.

In addition to pure water, vodkas can be born from a variety of ingredients. However, high-quality vodkas are generally distilled from a single source such as wheat, rye or potatoes. Once the choice of raw ingredients is made, the production of vodka is a reductive process whereby impurities and pain-causing congeners are removed. The more times vodka is distilled and filtered the greater its purity. So virtually all premium vodkas are distilled three or more times and painstakingly filtered.

The finest vodkas, when cold, have a subtle sweet or delicate grainy aroma – never a crude alcohol smell. Held up to the light, chilled vodka will have a milky luminescence and a velvety texture – with possibly a faint yellowish or bluish lustre.

As for flavour, fine chilled vodka should never taste harsh or bitter. Rather, it should have a smooth, crisp taste – never watery. Wheat vodkas are generally cleaner and smoother to the palate; rye vodkas are more robust, while potato vodkas tend to have a slightly creamy texture. Try sipping the vodka rather than shooting it. And you should compare different vodkas to more easily discern the nuances of each and arrive at the vodka you most prefer.

By all means, try vodka with different foods. Russians nearly always accompany vodka with salty dishes of potato or seafood. There is even an old, though hardly elegant, custom of holding a slice of Russian black bread up to the nose and inhaling as vodka is consumed – though no one seems to know exactly why. Probably this custom began when Russian vodkas were not properly distilled or filtered, and consequently were much harsher to imbibe.

Most important, regardless of your vodka preferences, always remember to deliver an appropriate toast before taking your first sip. Because, as any Russian will tell you, nothing will make the vodka taste better than a heartfelt toast among cheerful company.

COOKING

I am surprised more people don't use vodka, or any spirit for that matter, to impart or enhance flavours in foods. After all, alcohol is a common by-product that occurs in nature through fermentation. Man has used this chemical process to concentrate and intensify fruit essence into wines and spirits for centuries. It is even integral to the leavening process, which causes batter and dough to rise. Alcohol also enables many foods to release their flavours. The finest extracts (vanilla, for example) owe their intensity to alcohol. And spirits have also been used throughout the ages to cure meat and fish, as well as to preserve fruit and cakes.

Vodka is arguably superior to other spirits for cooking and infusing for the same reason it makes such a popular cocktail mixer. It can do everything other spirits can do and more. It can blend and enhance other flavours without altering their taste or it can be infused with any number of ingredients to create entirely new flavours.

In some recipes in this book, vodka is used to achieve a chemical reaction in a dish. As a marinade, for instance, it can help to tenderise meat by breaking down tough fibres. Vodka can also be used to braise meats and thereby soften and emulsify flavourings. Vodka added to cheese and cream sauces lowers the boiling point to help prevent curdling. It is also very effectively used to deglaze pans in order to dissolve and impart alcohol-soluble flavour compounds to foods or sauces. And sometimes vodka can provide a last-minute burst of flavour, or enhance the presentation of a dish – as in a flambé.

Exactly how much alcohol remains in a finished dish depends on the cooking method and duration. But, as a rule, those cooked at higher temperatures over a longer period will retain less alcohol. According to studies by the US Department of Agriculture, less than half of the original alcohol content will remain in a dish simmered for only 15 minutes; less than 25 per cent after 1 hour. In fact, some of the alcohol content will evaporate naturally during preparation or storage – without applying heat. Even the size of the pan can affect alcohol retention: the larger the pot, the greater the surface area, hence faster evaporation.

Uncooked foods containing vodka, or dishes where vodka is added just before serving, will retain nearly all their alcohol. And, surprisingly, a flambé may burn off only about 25 per cent of its alcohol content (due to the fact that a spirit must have a sufficiently high proportion of alcohol to water in order to burn). But a cup of vodka in a long-simmered soup or stew will give up most of its alcohol; though it will leave a legacy of intensified flavour.

Some among you may be disappointed to learn that once you factor in the cooking method and the proportion of vodka to the other ingredients, then divide by the number of servings, the alcohol content of many dishes in this book will be negligible. Add to that the fact that the consumption of food with spirits considerably slows the absorption rate of alcohol into the bloodstream. Lastly, when you consider that in many countries a food may be labelled 'non-alcoholic' and still contain nearly 1 per cent alcohol, it becomes obvious that many vodka dishes should provide little cause for concern.

COOKING WITH ALCOHOL

COOKING METHOD	ALCOHOL RETAINED
No heat, stored overnight	70 per cent
Stirred into hot liquid	85 per cent
Flamed	75 per cent
Not stirred in, baked for 25 min.	45 per cent
Stirred in, then baked or simmered for:	
15 minutes	40 per cent
30 minutes	35 per cent
1 hour	25 per cent
1½ hours	20 per cent
2 hours	10 per cent
2½ hours	5 per cent

SOURCE: United States Department of Agriculture

BRUNCH

is something deliciously decadent about brunch – preceded by the guilty pleas
ing in'. The meal should be novel or somewhat more elaborate than our
fast on-the-run and it should contain an eye-opener – usually in the form of a B
(you'll find my version on page 151), champagne or wine. But why not enliver
by incorporating a little vodka right into the dish? Go on. You know you wan
All the recipes in this section are breakfast-like creations. If you wish to put a little
in your brunch, just dig deeper into the book and cull dishes from other cho
is the one dining occasion when there are no rules. Breakfast, lunch, cocktails,
essert can all share the same table without quarrelling. Anything goes.
And since the hour is neither too early nor too late, why not make a day of it?
of food and some vodka on hand (and perhaps the Sunday newspapers and

BAKED VODKA GRAPEFRUIT

Vodka and grapefruit are a natural combination. Use this as a brunch starter or simply serve alongside a humble plate of eggs and bacon.

Serves 4
2 fresh grapefruit, halved
75ml (3fl oz) vodka
4 tablespoons sugar
Mint, to garnish

1 Preheat the oven to 150°C/300°F/gas mark 2.
2 Using a sharp serrated knife (or double-serrated grapefruit knife), section the fruit in each grapefruit half and allow a little of the juice to drain from each half. Replace this juice with about 1 tablespoon of the vodka.
3 Distribute the sugar evenly over the surface of each grapefruit half and place them in a baking tray.
4 Put the tray on the top shelf of the oven and bake until the sugar caramelises – about 8–10 minutes.
5 Serve immediately, garnished with mint.

Go ahead and cook this dish in a frying pan if you're in a rush. But for this recipe I prefer the double-boiler method to cook the eggs at a steady temperature without searing. The result is a smoother, creamier texture.

Serves 4

4 tablespoons chopped hot cherry
    peppers or jalapeño chillies
3 tablespoons vodka
8 fresh eggs
Salt and freshly ground black pepper,
    to taste
1 tablespoon chopped fresh basil
2 tablespoons sour cream
2 tablespoons butter
4 *Over-heated Tomatoes* (see page 33),
    chopped
Basil sprigs, to garnish

1 Marinate the chopped peppers in the vodka in a small bowl or jar for 1–2 hours.

2 Whisk the eggs in a medium bowl, with the salt, black pepper and chopped basil. Set aside.

3 In a third bowl, whip the sour cream with the vodka from the marinated peppers.

4 Melt the butter in a saucepan resting on a pan of simmering water.

5 Add the egg mixture, stirring constantly with a wooden spoon until almost firm – about 2–3 minutes.

6 Add the sour cream/vodka mixture to the eggs and stir.

7 Add the chopped peppers and *Over-heated Tomatoes*. Place on warm plates, garnish with basil sprigs and serve with tortilla chips (or toasted wedges of *Moscow Fry Bread*, see page 128) and *Roasted Pepper Salsa à la Vodka* (see page 129).

How can you tell if an egg is fresh? Don't hold me to this, but I have been told that it is possible to determine freshness by gently lowering an uncooked egg into a bowl of cold water. If the egg settles horizontally, it is fresh enough for human consumption. If it settles vertically, feed it to the dog. If it rises to the top, feed it to the plants. Of course, you could just look for the date stamped on the egg or packaging, but what would be the challenge in that?

MIXED-UP

EGGS

(Scrambled Eggs with Vodka
Peppers and Over-heated Tomatoes)

RUSSIAN TOAST WITH BANANAS FLAMBÉ AND RASPBERRY-LIME VODKA SAUCE

How do you make a Russian toast? Just hand him a glass of vodka. But seriously, folks... Russian toast is like French toast that knows how to party. There is vodka in three stages of this recipe. Plus you get to set it on fire. What could be more fun than that? And the recipe is easily doubled or trebled if you have a crowd to please.

Serves 4

2 eggs

2 teaspoons sugar

⅛ teaspoon salt

1 teaspoon *Vanilla Vodka* (see page 143) or vanilla extract

4 thick (about 2.5cm/1in) slices of dense bread, cut diagonally to make 8 triangular half slices

250ml (9fl oz) vodka

2 tablespoons butter

4 tablespoons brown sugar

2 bananas, thickly sliced

Raspberry-lime Vodka Sauce (see recipe below), warmed

125ml (4fl oz) crème fraîche or ricotta cheese

1 lime, cut into wedges, to serve

1 Whisk the eggs in a shallow bowl with the sugar, salt and *Vanilla Vodka*.

2 Lay the bread slices in a large dish or platter and pour about half the vodka over them.

3 Melt half the butter in a heavy-bottomed frying pan over a moderate-high heat. Cooking in batches, dip 3–4 vodka-soaked bread slices into the egg mixture and place in the frying pan. (Be sure to cover the slices completely with egg, but do not allow the egg to soak completely through the bread or it may break apart.)

4 Cook the slices until medium brown on both sides – about 2–3 minutes each side. The slices should be crisp on the surface, but tender inside. When ready, cover to keep warm and set aside. Repeat with the rest of the bread.

5 Add the remaining butter and brown sugar to the pan. As soon as the sugar has completely melted, add the sliced bananas and cook until slightly tender and coated in the butter/sugar mixture – about 1 minute. Add the remaining vodka to the pan and ignite (stand clear!).

6 Immediately top two slices of toast per plate with some of the bananas flambé and drizzle with *Raspberry-lime Vodka Sauce*. Add a large dollop of crème fraîche or ricotta and a lime wedge. Serve to applause.

RASPBERRY-LIME VODKA SAUCE

450g (1lb) fresh raspberries, or defrosted frozen raspberries

2 tablespoons *Vodka Simple Syrup* (see page 129)

3 tablespoons freshly squeezed lime juice

Grated zest of 1 lime

3 tablespoons *Lemon Peel Vodka* (see page 142)

Combine all the ingredients in a blender or food-processor, pulse to a chunky mixture and store in a glass jar in the fridge until needed. Raspberry-lime Vodka Sauce will keep for about a week in the fridge.

GRILLED SWEET POTATO TACOS WITH VODKA CHILLI MAPLE GLAZE

An American Southwest-inspired dish that has become one of my favourite breakfast items – especially when breakfast begins after noon.

Makes 4

1 tablespoon butter

4 tablespoons extra-virgin olive oil

450g (1lb) sweet potatoes, peeled and chopped

110g (4oz) onions, finely chopped

¼ teaspoon ground cinnamon

¼ teaspoon grated nutmeg

Salt and freshly ground black pepper

225g (8oz) cheddar cheese, grated

225g (8oz) mozzarella cheese, grated

4 circles *Moscow Fry Bread* (see page 128) or flour tortillas

1 tablespoon cayenne pepper

125ml (4fl oz) maple syrup

3 tablespoons vodka

1 teaspoon *KGB Sauce* (see page 124) or hot red pepper sauce

1 Preheat the oven to 150°C/300°F/gas mark 2.

2 Melt the butter with 2 tablespoons of the oil in a large frying pan over a moderate heat and sauté the sweet potatoes and onions. Cook until the potatoes are brown at the edges and cooked through – about 10 minutes. Dust with the cinnamon, nutmeg and salt and pepper to taste.

3 Divide the cheese between the circles of *Moscow Fry Bread* (or tortillas) and top with a portion of sweet potatoes.

4 Fold the bread in half over the filling, brush lightly with the remaining oil and sprinkle with cayenne pepper. Transfer to a baking tray and bake until crisp and the cheese has melted – about 5 minutes. Transfer to serving plates.

5 Combine the maple syrup, vodka and *KGB Sauce* in a small bowl and drizzle over the tacos.

6 Serve with fresh fruit or *Fermented Fruit* (see recipe below).

FERMENTED FRUIT

Your average fruit cocktail is a bit of a let-down. Sure it has fruit. But where's the cocktail? I fixed that.

Serves 2–4

110g (4oz) strawberries

110g (4oz) blueberries

110g (4oz) raspberries

110g (4oz) banana slices

125ml (4fl oz) freshly squeezed orange juice

4 tablespoons *Lemon Peel Vodka* (see page 142)

2 tablespoons sugar

1 Combine all the ingredients and mix well.

2 Chill and serve.

VODKA CRÊPES

This is a great brunch dish that is easy to prepare and allows for many variations according to the preferences of your guests. I usually cook all the crêpes in advance and then return them to the pan one at a time to create 'crêpes to order'. A selection of vodka crêpe fillings follows this basic recipe.

Makes about 16–18 crêpes

3 eggs

125g (4½oz) plain flour, sifted

2 teaspoons sugar

⅛ teaspoon salt

⅛ teaspoon freshly ground black pepper

2 tablespoons unsalted butter, melted

225ml (8fl oz) milk

4 tablespoons vodka

Vegetable oil

Filling of your choice (see below)

1 Combine the eggs, flour, sugar, salt and pepper in a medium bowl until the mixture is smooth.

2 Stir in the butter, milk and vodka to create a thin batter. Leave to rest for about 15–20 minutes.

3 Lightly oil a crêpe pan over a moderate heat. Pour about 2 tablespoons of the batter into the centre of the pan and quickly spread over the entire surface by tilting the pan with a circular motion from left to right. Cook the crêpe until the edges begin to brown, then flip and cook until done. Remove to a covered warm plate and repeat with the remaining batter.

4 When ready to serve, return one crêpe to the pan, add your choice of filling (see below), then fold the crêpe twice into a wedge shape and serve.

APPLE VODKA CRÊPE

Makes 1 crêpe

1 crêpe

1 tablespoon sugar

2 tablespoons *Apple Vodka* (see page 143)

⅛ teaspoon ground cinnamon

Return the crêpe to the warm pan and drizzle the sugar over the entire surface followed by the *Apple Vodka*. Quickly fold as described above, dust with cinnamon and serve.

CHOCOLATE VODKA CRÊPE

Makes 1 crêpe

1 crêpe

2 tablespoons *Chocolate Walnut Vodka* (see page 146)

1 dollop *Vodka Whipped Cream* (see page 119)

Return the crêpe to the warm pan and spread the *Chocolate Walnut Vodka* over the entire surface using the back of a spoon. Quickly fold as described above, top with the *Vodka Whipped Cream* and serve.

LEMON PEEL VODKA CRÊPE

Makes 1 crêpe

1 crêpe

1 tablespoon sugar

2 tablespoons *Lemon Peel Vodka* (see page 142)

1 lemon wedge

Return the crêpe to the warm pan and drizzle the sugar over the entire surface followed by the *Lemon Peel Vodka*. Quickly fold as described above and serve with the lemon wedge.

EGGS BENEDICT WITH VODKA CITRUS CHILLI HOLLANDAISE SAUCE

A classic brunch item has finally reached the legal drinking age. The real secret to poached eggs is to use very fresh eggs. The older the eggs, the more the loose albumen (egg white) will spread to create misshapen pouches or allow the yolk to seep out. Vodka Citrus Chilli Hollandaise Sauce can be kept warm by resting the bowl in warm (not hot) water.

Makes 8

8 *Sausage Patties* (see page 103), or
    Italian sausage
4 tablespoons butter, softened
4 English muffins, split in half
1 teaspoon white vinegar
Salt, to taste
8 very fresh eggs

Vodka Citrus Chilli Hollandaise Sauce

4 egg yolks
2 teaspoons freshly squeezed lemon juice
2 tablespoons *Lemon Peel Vodka* (see
    page 142)
½ teaspoon *KGB Sauce* (see page 124) or
    hot red pepper sauce
½ teaspoon freshly ground white pepper
110g (4oz) butter, melted and warmed
Parsley, to garnish

1 Prepare the *Sausage Patties* and form into flat rounds (or remove the sausages from their casings, flatten into patties and fry in oil over a moderate heat until cooked through) and set aside.

2 Butter the muffins and grill under a high heat until golden. Set aside.

3 Half-fill a large shallow pan with water, add a dash of vinegar and salt and bring to the boil. Crack 4 of the eggs into 4 small teacups. Holding 2 cups in each hand by the handles, gently lower the cups into the water and let the eggs float out. Immediately cover the pan, remove from the heat and cook the eggs for 3 minutes. Carefully remove the eggs from the pan with a slotted spoon and drain on a paper-lined plate. Season the eggs with salt and pepper. Return the pan to the heat and repeat.

4 Meanwhile, in a stainless-steel bowl set over a pan of gently simmering water, whisk the egg yolks with the lemon juice, *Lemon Peel Vodka*, *KGB Sauce* and white pepper until pale yellow and slightly thick. (Do not let the bowl touch the water.) Salt to taste. Remove the bowl from the pan and continue whisking while you slowly add the warm melted butter, until all is incorporated.

5 To assemble, place a sausage patty and egg on each muffin. Top with *Vodka Citrus Chilli Hollandaise Sauce* and garnish with parsley. Serve immediately with *Fermented Fruit* (see page 22) or *Baked Vodka Grapefruit* (see page 18).

Makes about 12

310g (11oz) flour, plus extra for working
    the dough
7g (¼oz) easy-blend yeast
½ teaspoon salt
4 tablespoons sugar
125ml (4fl oz) lukewarm still mineral water
4 tablespoons vodka
1 teaspoon *Vanilla Vodka* (see page 143)
    or vanilla extract
125ml (4fl oz) extra-virgin olive oil
2 eggs, beaten
1 litre (1¾ pints) vegetable oil, for frying
Vodka Ginger Pear Filling (recipe below)
Icing sugar, for dusting

GINGER PEAR FILLING

4 ripe pears, peeled, cored and finely
    chopped
110g (4oz) sugar
40g (1½oz) fresh ginger, finely chopped
125ml (4fl oz) vodka
1 tablespoon lemon juice
125ml (4fl oz) still mineral water

1 Combine all the ingredients in a large saucepan (do not use aluminium) and bring to the boil. Continue to boil, stirring frequently, for 20 minutes or until the mixture thickens.

2 Let the mixture cool, then inject into the doughnuts.

LOADED DOUGHNUTS (with Ginger Pear Filling)

It's easier than you might think to make fresh doughnuts at home. And you can't get these babies at the local doughnut shop.

1 Sift the flour into a large bowl. Add the yeast, salt and sugar and mix well.
2 Add the water, vodka, *Vanilla Vodka*, olive oil (reserving about 1 tablespoon for step 4) and eggs. Slowly mix until a smooth, sticky dough develops. Add more flour as necessary until you are able to form the dough into a loose ball and transfer it to a work surface covered with more flour. You want the dough to be as sticky as possible, yet still be able to work it.
3 Knead the dough on the work surface by repeatedly folding it and pressing it firmly into the flour-dusted surface using the heel of your hand. Form the dough into a ball and let it rest for a few minutes.
4 Grease a large bowl with the remaining olive oil and place the ball of dough in it. Roll the dough ball around the bottom of the bowl until it is lightly coated with the oil. (Sop up excess oil with kitchen paper if necessary.) Cover the bowl with a clean dry tea-towel, set aside in a warm place (away from draughts) and leave the dough to rise until it has doubled in volume – at least 2 hours. (The dough can be prepared the night before.)
5 Knead the dough again and, using a rolling pin, roll it out to a thickness of about 2cm (¾in). Cut into 8cm (about 3in) rounds with a cutter (or the rim of a jar or can). Cover the rounds with clean tea-towel and leave to rise for 1 hour.
6 Heat the vegetable oil in a heavy deep-sided pan until a 2.5cm (1in) cube of day-old bread browns in 30 seconds. Fry the rounds of dough (in batches as necessary) until golden brown. Drain on kitchen paper and leave to cool.
7 Inject with *Ginger Pear Filling* using a piping bag or spoon, then dust with icing sugar and serve.

STARTERS

Starters, appetisers, hors d'oeuvres, nibbles... whatever you like to call them, these little dishes are a great way to launch a vodka dinner. Or they can just as well stand on their own as 'small bites' or party fare. Russians nearly always accompany vodka with zakuski

There's lots of crunch and flavour in every bite of this twist on an Italian classic. I think bruschetta is as much about texture as flavour. I used to make the mistake of simply toasting the bread. The result was often a dry, crumbly foundation for the topping – most of which ended up on my shirt. Now I make the extra effort to fry the bread so the centre stays soft (and my laundry bills stay low). I find it equally important to chop everything meticulously to approximately the same size so that every spoonful of topping contains an equal share of all the ingredients. And lastly, a pinch of kosher salt just before serving adds a little explosion of saltiness as it hits the tongue.

Makes 20–24

5 tablespoons extra-virgin olive oil
1 fresh French baguette, cut into 2cm
     (¾in) slices
6 plum tomatoes, finely chopped
2 small spring onions, finely chopped
4 tablespoons green olives, finely
     chopped
40g (1½oz) basil leaves, finely chopped
3 tablespoons *Basil Vodka* (see page 146)
     or vodka
1 tablespoon vermouth
1 teaspoon freshly ground black pepper
2–3 garlic cloves
1 tablespoon kosher salt or coarse sea salt
Basil sprigs, to garnish

1 Warm 3 tablespoons of the olive oil in a large heavy-bottomed frying pan over a moderate heat. Gently fry the bread slices until just golden on each side (but the centres are still soft) and set aside.

2 Combine and mix the rest of the oil with the tomatoes, spring onions, green olives, chopped basil, *Basil Vodka* or vodka, vermouth and black pepper in a large bowl. Cover and set aside.

3 When ready to serve, bruise the cloves of garlic (by giving them a whack with a rolling pin or the flat side of a chef's knife) and rub onto each toast. Discard the garlic. Add a spoonful of the tomato mixture and a pinch of kosher or sea salt to each toast. Serve on a platter garnished with sprigs of basil.

For an extra kick, add 1–2 teaspoons of *KGB Sauce* (see page 124), or hot red pepper sauce to the tomato mixture.

DISTILLED

BRUSCHETTA

MARTINI PIZZETTA FLAMBÉ

Here's a unique small stovetop white pizza (no tomatoes) recipe that brings new meaning to the term 'Martini lunch'. This pizzetta is made very quickly in just one pan, using Moscow Fry Bread for a thin crispy crust.

Makes 4

125ml (4fl oz) extra-virgin olive oil

250g (9oz) white onions, chopped

1 teaspoon crushed garlic (about 2 cloves)

225g (8oz) green olives, halved and marinated in 125ml (4fl oz) vodka for about 3 hours

1 tablespoon vermouth

1 teaspoon sugar

½ teaspoon freshly ground white pepper

½ teaspoon salt

4 circles Moscow Fry Bread (see page 128)

350g (12oz) mozzarella, grated

110g (4oz) fresh mild green chillies, chopped

4 tablespoons vodka

Shredded basil, to garnish

1 Heat 3 tablespoons of the olive oil in a heavy frying pan over a moderate-low heat. Cook the onions and garlic for about 10 minutes until soft, stirring frequently to prevent them browning.

2 Drain the vodka from the olives (reserving the olives) and add it to the onions along with the vermouth, sugar, white pepper and salt. Simmer until the onions have absorbed all the liquid. Then pulse in a blender or food processor until smooth. Rinse the pan and return to moderate-high heat.

3 Roll out a circle of Moscow Fry Bread as described on page 128 and add to the pan with 1 tablespoon of the oil. As soon as the edges turn golden, flip it over and spoon a generous amount of the vodka onion sauce onto the centre of the bread. Then, using the bottom of the spoon, 'paint' the sauce onto the bread in a circular pattern from the middle to the edge until you have covered the surface.

4 Again starting from the middle, distribute the mozzarella cheese evenly over the surface. Top with about a teaspoon of chillies and evenly distribute the olive halves.

5 Cover the pan and cook the pizzetta for about 2–3 minutes, or until all the cheese has melted. Remove the lid and continue to cook until the bread is crisp – about another 4–5 minutes.

6 Drizzle with about a tablespoon of vodka and ignite with a flame from the gas burner, a chef's blowtorch or a long wooden match. Slide the pizzetta onto a warm plate and serve immediately, garnished with shredded basil. Repeat to make each pizzetta.

It should go without saying that every precaution should be taken when using an open flame in your home. Be sure to have a fire extinguisher nearby and keep clear of other flammable objects like clothing, curtains, or your mother-in-law.

ABOUT CAVIAR

If you're going to serve caviar, you should probably know a little something about it.

Russia produces the finest and most sought-after caviars in the world from the roe of three types of sturgeon found in the Caspian Sea.

The three types of Russian caviar are named after the sturgeon from which the roe is harvested: Beluga (the world's most prized and expensive large-egg caviar), Ossetra and Sevruga. Beluga caviar is pearl-grey in colour and has a smooth, buttery flavour. Ossetra is warm brown to greenish-grey with a delicate taste and firm grain. Sevruga caviar is black-grey in tone with a strong taste and small grain.

Caviar should be maintained at about 2°C (35°F), colder than a fridge but not quite as cold as a freezer (try the back of your fridge). If handled properly, an unopened container of caviar will stay fresh for a couple of months. However, once opened, fresh caviar must be consumed within a few days.

Fresh caviar is very expensive because it requires special care of the roe – which can only be harvested from 'mature' fish between 5 and 15 years of age – in order to yield eggs of the proper size and texture. In addition, over-fishing and pollution in the Caspian Sea have caused a dramatic drop in the numbers of these prehistoric fish. This has led to a reduction in the production and availability – and a rise in price – of sturgeon caviar in Russia and other countries. In fact, as I write this, Beluga sturgeon may soon find their way onto the endangered species list. Please buy caviar only from reputable purveyors, and let's hope that a solution is found to keep a sustainable supply of caviar available for generations to come.

STRAIGHT-UP VODKA AND CAVIAR

Vodka and caviar go together like... well... like vodka and caviar. Travelling frequently from Russia to Europe and the USA, I have often brought along fresh Russian caviar as gifts to friends and family. However, I have discovered that since many people have never even tasted caviar and rarely purchase this Russian delicacy, they are often unsure about how to serve it.

In Russia, where caviar is a staple and more affordable than in the West, it is not uncommon for it to be served a lot like jam – piled onto a buttered slice of Russian black bread or plain toast. Russians like their caviar just as they like their vodka: simple and unadorned.

But for most of us, caviar is a rare treat. So I believe that more time and attention should be put into its presentation and consumption. The impact and enjoyment of this dish is greatly enhanced through presentation and ritual. Here's how I like to serve it.

Serves 2

2 hard-boiled eggs
2 shallots, finely chopped
4 tablespoons whipped unsalted butter or crème fraîche
1 French baguette, thinly sliced and lightly toasted
50g (2oz) fresh Russian Beluga, Ossetra or Sevruga caviar
½ lemon, cut into small wedges
Vodka, chilled (of course), to serve

1 Shell the eggs, halve carefully and remove the solid yolks. Finely chop the whites separately from the yolks. Place each into separate sections of a partitioned serving dish or in two small serving dishes. In the remaining sections or two further small serving dishes distribute the shallots and butter or crème fraîche.

2 Serve the toasted bread slices in a napkin-lined basket or bowl.

3 Keep the caviar in its jar or tin and nestle it in a larger bowl filled with crushed ice. Surround the caviar dish with the tiny lemon wedges.

4 Supply a non-metallic spoon – traditionally made from horn, bone or mother-of-pearl – for serving the caviar. (Never use silver as it imparts a metallic taste and the caviar will discolour the silver.)

5 Finally, have plenty of chilled vodka on hand – ideally kept champagne-style in an ice-filled bucket – and serve in chilled shot or aperitif glasses.

6 Invite your guests to serve themselves by spooning caviar (carefully to avoid crushing the eggs) onto a lightly buttered slice of toasted bread and adding a squeeze of lemon, followed by any combination of the remaining ingredients they wish – followed by a sip of chilled vodka.

In addition to the presentation above, caviar can be enjoyed with fresh or grilled oysters, scrambled eggs or as a garnish atop soups, potatoes, pasta, salad, seafood, or (boiled, shelled and halved) quail's eggs.

HALF-IN-THE-BAG CHICKEN WINGS

'Half in the bag' means something else where I come from. But in this case it refers to the chicken. Whether you're having a party, or just want to pretend you are, these wings will be a sure-fire hit. I like to use a plastic bag rather than a bowl to marinate the chicken. It makes it easier to coat the wings thoroughly using less marinade, takes up less space in my fridge and I can travel to a cookout or party with nothing to wash or carry home. Just be sure to trim the tips off the wings using kitchen shears or you risk puncturing the bag. And that would be bad – for the chicken and your shoes.

Makes 24

12 chicken wings, halved at the joint, rinsed, tips removed

110g (4oz) onions, finely chopped

4 tablespoons *Orange Peel Vodka* (see page 142) or vodka

4 tablespoons orange marmalade

2 tablespoons *KGB Sauce* (see page 124), or hot pepper sauce

1 tablespoon Worcestershire sauce

2 tablespoons freshly squeezed lemon juice

1 tablespoon crushed garlic (about 8 cloves)

1 tablespoon red wine vinegar

¼ tablespoon Dijon mustard

1 teaspoon salt

½ teaspoon freshly ground black pepper

1 Place the wings in a large resealable plastic bag (or plastic container). Add the remaining ingredients, seal the bag and shake to coat the wings.
2 Refrigerate for at least 6 hours and up to 24 hours – turning the bag occasionally.
3 Preheat the oven to 190°C/375°F/gas mark 5.
4 Drain the chicken wings, reserving the marinade. Place the wings on a baking tray. Bake for 45–60 minutes, brushing occasionally with the marinade. Stop adding the marinade at least 5 minutes before removing from the oven. Alternatively you could just toss these wings on a hot barbecue grill, turning until cooked through.

If you want to serve the remaining marinade as a dipping sauce, be sure to bring it to the boil in a small saucepan over a high heat for several minutes to ensure it is bacteria-free.

VODKA-STEAMED PRAWN COCKTAIL

Steaming with vodka seems to impart a subtle nutty flavour to the prawns. And the resulting broth is used to perk up the cocktail sauce.

Serves 4

125ml (4fl oz) vodka

2 bay leaves

1 teaspoon salt

24 raw whole tiger prawns, rinsed

225ml (8fl oz) *Vodka and Onion Ketchup* (see page 125)

2 tomatoes, seeded and very finely chopped

2 tablespoons grated horseradish

1 tablespoon *KGB Sauce* (see page 124)

2 tablespoons *Lemon Peel Vodka* (see page 142)

1 teaspoon finely chopped coriander leaves

Freshly ground black pepper, to taste

4 lettuce leaves

4 lemon wedges, to garnish

1 Bring the vodka, bay leaves, salt and 125ml (4fl oz) water to a rapid boil in a large covered saucepan.

2 Add the prawns to the water, cover and steam for 3–5 minutes or until the prawns turn pink. DO NOT DRAIN THE LIQUID.

3 Remove the prawns from the pan with a slotted spoon and leave to cool. Set aside the liquid in the pan. Once the prawns have cooled to room temperature, peel, de-vein and transfer to an airtight container. Refrigerate for at least 3 hours.

4 Remove the bay leaves from the reserved liquid and boil until it is reduced to about 4 tablespoons.

5 Strain this liquid into a bowl along with the remaining ingredients (apart from the lettuce leaves and lemon wedges) and mix into a chunky sauce. Chill in the fridge in a closed container for at least 2 hours.

6 When ready to serve, lay a lettuce leaf on top of a martini glass, add a heaped tablespoon of the cocktail sauce and position 6 prawns around the rim – with the meaty end of the prawns embedded in the sauce. Add a lemon wedge to garnish and serve.

If you have a large supply of shot glasses, you can make fewer prawns go further at larger gatherings by adding cocktail sauce and 1 or 2 prawns to each glass with a tiny wedge of lemon.

FOOD

FLIGHTS

Where do drinks end and foods begin? These liquescent nibbles blur the line. Served as appetisers, soup courses or just about anywhere during a meal, Food Flights pack a lot of flavour (but not a lot of alcohol) into a few sips. Presented in shot glasses, one or more of these soupy shooters are an ideal way to introduce or complement a vodka dining theme.

Borrowed from the vernacular of those who conduct wine or spirit-tastings, 'flights' are small servings presented together in order that the taster may compare and contrast their various attributes. In much the same manner, I often serve several Food Flights together at the beginning of a meal as a novel and colourful starter – sort of a tasting menu, served neat. If you have plenty of glasses, Food Flights also make for festive hors d'oeuvres at even the largest of gatherings. No forks, no plates, no toothpicks mean no fuss, no mess and a lot less clean-up.

VODKA PIZZA FLIGHT

Sounds weird, huh? But believe it or not, this recipe packs all the flavour of a slice of pizza – into a shot glass. Just close your eyes, drink the shot and take a bite of bread stick or focaccia. You'll thank me.

Makes 8–10

450ml (16fl oz) *Vodka Tomato Sauce* (see page 100)

4 tablespoons vodka

2 tablespoons grated Parmesan-Reggiano

2 teaspoons finely chopped fresh basil

2 teaspoons sugar

8–10 balls fresh buffalo mozzarella, each approximately 2.5cm (1in) across

8–10 basil leaves (with stems) to garnish

8–10 bread sticks or small wedges of focaccia

Crushed red chilli flakes (optional)

1 Warm the *Vodka Tomato Sauce*, vodka, Parmesan, chopped basil and sugar in a small saucepan over a moderate heat, until the Parmesan melts and is completely incorporated – about 5 minutes. Transfer to a blender or food-processor and whizz to a smooth purée.

2 Pour the mixture into tall shot glasses. Float a ball of mozzarella on the top of each glass and tuck in a basil leaf. Serve warm, but not hot, with breadsticks or focaccia. Sprinkle a dash of crushed red chilli flakes on top if you like it spicy.

CHILLED CHERRY VODKA CITRUS FLIGHT

This one can handily start or end any meal.

Makes 10–12

450g (1lb) sour red cherries, stoned

4 tablespoons *Sour Cherry Vodka* (see page 146)

125ml (4fl oz) dry white wine

3 tablespoons sugar

2 tablespoons fresh lemon juice

125ml (4fl oz) sour cream, plus 10–12 spoonfuls for topping

1 tablespoon grated lemon zest

Mint sprigs, to garnish

1 Steal 10–12 of the cherries, submerge them in the *Sour Cherry Vodka* and place in the fridge until needed.

2 Bring the remainder of the cherries, the wine, sugar and lemon juice to the boil in a medium saucepan over a high heat. Then reduce the heat and simmer the mixture until the cherries are very tender and the liquid has reduced by approximately a quarter – about 15–20 minutes.

3 Whizz the mixture in a blender or food-processor to a smooth purée. Allow to cool to room temperature, then cover and chill in the fridge for about 2–3 hours.

4 Whisk the 125ml (4fl oz) sour cream in a large mixing bowl to liquefy slightly. Then add the cherry mixture.

5 Remove the macerated cherries from the fridge and strain the vodka into the cherry and sour cream mixture, reserving the cherries. Stir.

6 Pour into chilled tall shot glasses, top with a small dollop of remaining plain sour cream, sprinkle with lemon zest, top with a macerated cherry and add a sprig of mint.

VODKA TOMATO CREAM FLIGHT

This creamy tomato shot and some crusty Italian bread usually keep everyone pacified until dinnertime.

Makes 10–12

450ml (16fl oz) *Vodka Tomato Sauce* (see page 100)

4 tablespoons vodka

4 tablespoons breadcrumbs

4 tablespoons finely chopped fresh basil

4 tablespoons double cream

Crusty bread, to serve

1 In a small saucepan over a moderate heat, warm the *Vodka Tomato Sauce*, vodka, breadcrumbs and 1 tablespoon of the basil. Transfer to a blender or food-processor and whizz to a smooth purée. Stir in the cream.

2 Pour the mixture into tall shot glasses. Garnish each glass with the remaining chopped basil. Serve warm, but not hot, with a small slice of crusty bread.

VODKA POTATO LEEK FLIGHT

This is a tasty in-between course to serve with or before a hearty meat or chicken dish. It may also be served cold, with a bit of cream stirred in, to make a refreshing summer starter – similar to a classic Vichyssoise.

Makes 10–12

2 tablespoons unsalted butter

225g (8oz) leeks, white portions only (save a few green leaves to garnish), thinly sliced and rinsed

600ml (1 pint) *Vodka Chicken Broth* (see page 126)

225g (8oz) potatoes, cut into even chunks

4 tablespoons vodka

Salt and freshly ground pepper

1 Melt the butter in a large saucepan over a moderate-high heat. Add the leeks and sauté until they soften – about 3–5 minutes.

2 Add the *Vodka Chicken Broth* and potatoes and bring to the boil. Reduce the heat to low, cover and simmer until the potatoes are very tender – about 20–25 minutes.

3 Whizz to a smooth purée in a blender or food-processor. Stir in the vodka and season to taste.

4 Serve warm, but not hot, in tall shot glasses. Cut thin ribbons from the green leaves of the leeks and use to garnish each glass.

If the flight becomes too thick, thin with warm milk and/or extra broth.

CURRIED PUMPKIN AND VODKA FLIGHT

Not since Cinderella has a pumpkin been imbued with so much 'get up and go'.

Makes 10–12

2 tablespoons unsalted butter

110g (4oz) onions, finely chopped

450g (1lb) fresh pumpkin, peeled, seeded and chopped

450ml (16fl oz) *Vodka Chicken Broth* (see page 126), warmed

1 bay leaf

1 teaspoon brown sugar

½ teaspoon curry powder

⅛ teaspoon grated nutmeg

1 teaspoon finely chopped parsley

4 tablespoons vodka

Salt and freshly ground white pepper

2 tablespoons roasted pumpkin seeds*

1 Melt the butter in a large saucepan over a moderate heat, add the onions and cook until translucent – about 3 minutes.

2 Reduce the heat to low, add the pumpkin, cover and cook until the pumpkin is tender – about 15 minutes.

3 Add the *Vodka Chicken Broth*, bay leaf, brown sugar, curry powder, nutmeg and parsley. Increase the heat to high and bring to the boil. Immediately reduce the heat to low and simmer, uncovered, for about 15 minutes.

4 Remove from the heat, discard the bay leaf, transfer to a blender or food-processor and whizz to a smooth purée. Add the vodka, salt and pepper to taste.

5 Serve warm, but not hot, in tall shot glasses. Add a few roasted pumpkin seeds to each glass.

If the flight becomes too thick to sip, thin with more broth.

For more tender, flavourful flesh, choose smaller pumpkins for cooking. They should be without large blemishes and, ideally, with their stems intact. They should feel weighty for their size. Fresh pumpkins may be stored in a cool, dry place for up to about 1 month before use.

*You can roast pumpkin seeds in a dry pan over a moderate heat. In order to cook them evenly and prevent burning, keep the pan moving over the heat and stir constantly with a wooden spoon. When the seeds begin to brown – after about 3–4 minutes – remove from the heat and let cool. Season to taste with salt and/or cayenne pepper.

OPPOSITE PAGE Chilled Vodka Borscht
Flight (top left and this page, right), Vodka
Roasted Red Pepper Flight (top right), Vodka
Carrot Flight (centre), Vodka Potato Leek
Flight (bottom and this page, left)

CHILLED VODKA BORSCHT FLIGHT

Contrary to popular belief, borscht actually originated in the Ukraine, not Russia – though it finds its way onto most Russian tables. Serve it chilled and pretend you're ice-fishing on the Moscow River.

Makes 10–12

450ml (16fl oz) *Vodka Beef Broth* (see page 127)

450g (1lb) beetroots, peeled and grated

1 bay leaf

½ teaspoon (or more to taste) *KGB Sauce* (see page 124) or hot pepper sauce

3 tablespoons freshly squeezed orange juice

125ml (4fl oz) sour cream

4 tablespoons vodka

Salt and freshly ground white pepper

1 cucumber, sliced and chilled to garnish

Sprigs of fresh dill to garnish

10–12 small squares of Russian black bread or dark rye, to serve

1 Bring the *Vodka Beef Broth*, beetroots, bay leaf and *KGB Sauce* to the boil in a medium saucepan over a moderate heat. Reduce the heat to low, cover and simmer for about 30 minutes. Remove from the heat, stir in the orange juice and leave to cool to room temperature.

2 Dispose of the bay leaf and chill in the fridge for 2–3 hours, or up to 2–3 days.

3 Before serving, skim off any solidified fat from the surface of the borscht. Then transfer to a blender or food-processor and whizz to a smooth purée.

4 In a mixing bowl, whisk about 4 tablespoons of the sour cream with the vodka until smooth. Add to the borscht and season to taste with salt and white pepper.

5 Place the cucumber slices on the rims of chilled tall shot glasses, add the borscht, a dollop of sour cream and a sprig of dill. Serve with a square of black bread.

VODKA ROASTED RED PEPPER FLIGHT

The marriage of roasted pepper and fennel makes this one of my favourite flights, and the one I'm most often asked to prepare.

Makes 10–12

2 large red peppers, quartered and seeded

4 tablespoons olive oil

110g (4oz) onions, finely sliced

50g (2oz) carrots, finely chopped

50g (2oz) fennel bulb, finely chopped

350ml (12fl oz) *Vodka Chicken Broth* (see page 126), warmed

4 tablespoons *Basil Vodka* (see page 146)

¼ teaspoon *KGB Sauce* (see page 124) or hot red pepper sauce

Salt and freshly ground black pepper

2–3 drops balsamic vinegar

10–12 slices of toasted bread, cut into 2.5cm (1in) squares

1 Lay the quartered peppers flat on a grill pan or baking tray – skin-side up – and brush with 2 tablespoons of the olive oil. Place under a hot grill until the skins blister and blacken – about 10–15 minutes. Remove from the heat and, when cool enough to handle, peel or scrape off the skin and cut the peppers into thin strips.

2 Add the remaining oil to a large deep-sided pan over a moderate-low heat and cook the onions, carrots and fennel until tender – about 10–15 minutes.

3 Stir in the *Vodka Chicken Broth*, *Basil Vodka* and *KGB Sauce*, add the grilled peppers and bring to the boil. Immediately reduce the heat and simmer, partially covered, for about 30 minutes.

4 Transfer the mixture to a blender or food-processor and whizz to a smooth purée.

5 Season with salt, pepper and balsamic vinegar. Serve warm, but not hot, in tall shot glasses with the small squares of toasted bread – ideally, rubbed with garlic and brushed with olive oil.

VODKA CARROT FLIGHT

This flight reminds me of an old joke: 'How do you make gold soup? Just use 24 carrots'. (I didn't say it was a funny joke.) This is no simple carrot juice cocktail. The aniseed and other ingredients distinguish this recipe from the rest and provide this flight with its surprising character.

Makes 10–12

2 tablespoons unsalted butter

110g (4oz) onions, thinly sliced

350g (12oz) carrots, thinly sliced

1 tablespoon brown sugar

1 teaspoon ground aniseed

450ml (16fl oz) *Vodka Chicken Broth* (see page 126)

4 tablespoons *Lemon Peel Vodka* (see page 142)

2 tablespoons freshly squeezed orange juice

2 tablespoons extra-virgin olive oil

1 teaspoon caraway seeds

Salt and freshly ground white pepper

2–3 slices toasted bread, cut into 1cm (½in) croûtons

1 Melt the butter in a large deep-sided pan over a moderate-high heat. Add the onions and sauté until they are translucent – about 5 minutes. Add the carrots, brown sugar and ground aniseed, reduce the heat to low, cover and cook for about 10 minutes.
2 Add the *Vodka Chicken Broth*, *Lemon Peel Vodka* and orange juice, raise the heat to high and bring to the boil. Immediately reduce the heat to low, cover and simmer until the carrots are very tender – about 15 minutes.
3 Meanwhile, heat the olive oil in a medium frying pan over a moderate-high heat. Add the caraway seeds and sauté for about 1 minute. Add the croûtons, stir until coated and golden – about 3 minutes – and set aside.
4 Transfer the carrot mixture to a blender or food-processor and whizz to a smooth purée.
5 Season to taste with salt and pepper. Serve warm, but not hot, in tall shot glasses. Add a few croûtons to each glass.

If the flight becomes too thick to sip, thin with more broth.

WARM BLOODY MARY FLIGHT

The Bloody Natasha recipe on page 151 can be warmed in a saucepan and served in shot glasses to make about 10–12 spicy shots. A classic in miniature, it's a novel way to get brunch (or any meal, for that matter) off to a bloody good start.

VODKA FRUIT FLIGHT

This flight makes a great palate-cleanser between dishes and is dead simple to prepare. You can use virtually any combination of available fresh fruits. But be sure to chop the fruits very finely to make the flight easy to sip (or slurp) from shot glasses.

Makes 10–12

110g (4oz) fresh or tinned pineapple, finely chopped

110g (4oz) fresh or tinned pears, peeled, cored and finely chopped

110g (4oz) apples, peeled, cored and finely chopped

125ml (4fl oz) freshly squeezed orange juice

125ml (4fl oz) *Lemon Peel Vodka* (see page 142)

2 tablespoons *Vodka Simple Syrup* (see page 129)

Ground cinnamon, to taste

Mint leaves, to garnish

1 Mix all the ingredients and chill.
2 Serve in chilled tall shot glasses, garnished with mint.

WATER WORKS

Water, purer than any spring, de-mineralised, de-ionised and filtered, is checked 7 times before being used in the production of Smirnoff vodka.

SALADS & SOUPS

Get ready for some well-dressed salads and a few souped-up soups. Vodka really shines in the following recipes. Its presence is especially felt in the salad dressings because most of them are uncooked – making the vodka more palpable (though not overpowering). One salad dressing is even served up in a cocktail shaker. This is one 'salad bar' you won't soon forget.

Spirits were added to soups, bisques and stews long before I began experimenting with vodka. And for good reason. Spirits add a welcome complexity to broth because they are more fully integrated into the dish. But whereas other spirits also impart specific flavours to the meal, vodka can be subtler. For example, I've used vodka to balance the creamy consistency of some soups and, in one case, add a little bite to a chilled soup. What's more, vodka accentuates the flavours in the Vodka Chicken Broth (see page 126) and Vodka Beef Broth (see page 127) used as a base for these soups. Both broths can also be enjoyed on their own without further embellishment.

This is a presentation piece – the spirits are added to the remainder of the dressing tableside and blended in a cocktail shaker. It's a great way to set the stage for a meal that will include several vodka-infused recipes.

Serves 4–6

Juice and grated zest of 1 large lemon
    (about 4 tablespoons juice;
    1 tablespoon zest)
4 tablespoons green olives, chopped
2 tablespoons white wine vinegar
4 tablespoons sour cream
3 tablespoons olive oil
½ tablespoon crushed garlic
Salt and freshly ground black pepper
Mixed salad leaves
4 tablespoons chilled vodka
2 tablespoons chilled dry vermouth
Green olives or pickled onions marinated
    in vodka, to garnish

1 Whizz the lemon juice in a blender or food-processor with the olives, vinegar, sour cream, olive oil, crushed garlic, salt and pepper.
2 Add the lemon zest and continue to pulse until smooth. Transfer to a large cocktail shaker, cover and refrigerate for at least 1 hour.
3 Wash the salad leaves, tear into bite-size pieces and share among 4–6 salad bowls.
4 Present at the table by adding the vodka and vermouth to the dressing in the cocktail shaker (approximate the amounts required as you pour straight from the bottle – bartender-style). Cover, shake and pour the dressing over the bowls of salad.
5 Garnish each bowl with 2–3 marinated green olives or pickled onions skewered on a cocktail stick – martini-style.

SHAKEN
NOT STIRRED SALAD

VODKA BLACK BEAN AND GRILLED SWEETCORN SALAD

This is an ideal summer side dish or a cool, flavourful complement to a spicy entrée.

Serves 8–10

450g (1lb) dried or tinned black beans

2 sweetcorn cobs

1 small pepper

4 tablespoons vodka

2 tablespoons freshly squeezed lime juice and the grated zest from the limes

125ml (4fl oz) olive oil

2 garlic cloves, crushed

1 teaspoon salt

1 teaspoon *KGB Sauce* (see page 124) or hot red pepper sauce

2 medium tomatoes, seeded and finely chopped

6 spring onions, finely chopped

1 fresh hot chilli, seeded and very finely chopped

110g (4oz) coriander, finely chopped

1 Soak the dried beans for 8–10 hours in cold water. Drain and rinse. If using tinned beans, simply drain and rinse before adding to the salad (step 6).

2 Put the beans into a large pot with enough fresh water to cover them by 2.5cm (1in).

3 Bring to the boil, then simmer over a low heat until the beans are barely tender – approximately 2 hours. Drain, rinse and cool.

4 Place the sweetcorn and pepper in a grill pan and grill until slightly brown, turning as necessary. Remove and trim the corn kernels from the cobs; skin, seed and chop the pepper.

5 Combine the vodka, lime juice and zest, olive oil, garlic, salt and *KGB Sauce* in a small bowl and mix well.

6 Combine the cooked beans, corn, pepper, tomatoes, spring onions, chilli and coriander in a salad bowl.

7 Pour the vodka mixture over the bean salad and toss until well coated. Refrigerate until ready to serve.

VODKA AND LEMON SWEET SHREDDED CARROTS

This makes a simple and refreshing side salad.

Serves 4–6

4 large carrots, chilled in the fridge for at least 2 hours

2 tablespoons freshly squeezed lemon juice

1 teaspoon grated lemon zest

3 tablespoons *Lemon Peel Vodka* (see page 142) or vodka

1 tablespoon sugar

¼ teaspoon salt

1 Peel and grate the carrots using a grater or mandolin.

2 Combine all the ingredients, toss well and serve.

VODKA TOMATO SALAD DRESSING WITH FRIED TOMATO SKINS

Tomato skins are fried tempura-style to create a crispy taste sensation to top this salsa-inspired salad dressing. (Try saying that five times fast.)

Serves 4–6

6 plum tomatoes

Salt and freshly ground black pepper

1 tablespoon chopped garlic

4 tablespoons chopped fresh basil

4 tablespoons red wine vinegar

2 tablespoons *Basil Vodka* (see page 146)

2 tablespoons extra-virgin olive oil

450ml (16fl oz) vegetable oil

2 tablespoons flour

Mixed salad leaves

4 tablespoons pitted black olives, halved

1 Wash and score the tops of the tomatoes with a cross and cook for 1 minute in enough boiling water to cover and ½ teaspoon salt. Remove the tomatoes and plunge into very cold water or ice to stop them from cooking.

2 Slip the tomatoes out of their skins – reserving the skins – and slice and de-seed. Mix together with the garlic, basil, vinegar, *Basil Vodka* and salt and pepper to taste in a blender or food-processor. Add the olive oil slowly while pulsing until the mixture is smooth. Refrigerate for at least 1 hour.

3 Meanwhile, heat the vegetable oil in a deep-sided pan over a high heat. Pat the tomato skins as dry as possible, roll them in the flour, gently shake off the excess and fry until crisp. (Be careful: the hot oil may splatter when the skins are added to the pan.) Drain on kitchen paper and lightly salt.

4 Wash the mixed salad leaves and tear into bite-size pieces; set aside.

5 Pour the salad dressing over the leaves, top with fried tomato skins and olive halves and serve.

The dressing will keep in an airtight container in the fridge for up to 2 weeks.

CHILLIES STUFFED WITH GOAT'S CHEESE AND DATES IN VODKA SWEET PEPPER SAUCE

I love the combination of spicy heat and sweetness in this dish. And the Vodka Sweet Pepper Sauce makes the intense flavours explode in your mouth. (Trust me: that's a good thing.)

Makes 4

4 large mild chillies (e.g. Anaheim or New Mexican Red)

6 rashers bacon, fried crisp and finely chopped

150g (5oz) soft goat's cheese

50g (2oz) pitted dates, finely chopped

1 teaspoon *KGB Sauce* (see page 124) or hot red pepper sauce

3 tablespoons extra-virgin olive oil

Mixed salad leaves

Vodka Sweet Pepper Sauce

110g (4oz) red pepper

2 tablespoons finely chopped onion

1 teaspoon very finely chopped fresh ginger

3 tablespoons freshly squeezed orange juice

4 tablespoons vodka

1 teaspoon grated orange zest

Salt, to taste

1 Preheat the oven to 200°C/400°F/gas mark 6.

2 Make a slit down one side of each chilli – leaving the stems intact (do not slice through) – and carefully remove the seeds and fibres using a spoon or paring knife.

3 Combine the bacon, goat's cheese, dates and *KGB Sauce* in a medium bowl and mix.

4 Stuff the cheese mixture into each chilli.

5 Arrange the chillies in a roasting tin, drizzle with 2 tablespoons of the olive oil and cover with aluminium foil. Cook in the oven until the chillies soften – about 30 minutes. Remove the foil and grill until the cheese mixture begins to brown – about 3–5 minutes.

6 Meanwhile, heat the remaining oil with the red pepper, onion and ginger in a medium saucepan over a moderate heat until the pepper softens – about 5 minutes. Pulse in a blender or food-processor with the orange juice, vodka and orange zest until a smooth, creamy sauce is formed. Add salt to taste (it should be slightly bitter).

7 To serve, lay some salad leaves on a small plate, place a stuffed chilli in the centre and drizzle with *Vodka Sweet Pepper Sauce*.

WARM VODKA SALAD WITH BACON AND GARLIC PARMESAN CROÛTONS

I find that the trick to keeping warm salads from turning limp is to use a very large frying pan, toss the mixed leaves quickly in the hot pan and serve.

Serves 4

4 tablespoons vodka

1 tablespoon crushed garlic

10g (½oz) butter, melted

1 French baguette, cut into bite-size cubes

110g (4oz) Parmesan-Reggiano, grated

Mixed salad leaves

8 rashers bacon, finely chopped

4 tablespoons cider vinegar

½ tablespoon fresh black peppercorns, crushed

1 teaspoon sugar

½ teaspoon *KGB Sauce* (see page 124), or hot red pepper sauce

1 Preheat the oven to 150°C/300°F/gas mark 2.

2 In a small bowl, combine 1 tablespoon of the vodka, garlic and butter. Lightly dip each bread cube into the vodka/butter mixture and then into the Parmesan, then lay on a baking tray, cheese-side up. Bake until crisp – about 3–5 minutes – and set aside.

3 Wash the salad leaves, tear into bite-size pieces and set aside.

4 In a large heavy frying pan, brown the bacon until very crisp.

5 Deglaze the pan with the vinegar, then add the peppercorns, sugar, *KGB Sauce* and remaining vodka and bring the mixture to the boil.

6 Immediately remove from the heat, add the mixed leaves to the pan and toss just long enough to coat – about 5 seconds. Serve family-style in a large salad bowl topped with the garlic-parmesan croûtons.

VODKA WHITE BEAN AND ROASTED GARLIC SOUP SERVED IN A ROASTED TOMATO

I love dishes where you can eat the container. It's kind of like eating the ice cream and then eating the cone. This Tuscan-inspired soup is served in large hollowed-out tomatoes (in Russia I use large tomatoes called 'bychie sertse', or 'bull's heart'). And, as you eat the soup, you can cut into the tomato as well. And the bacon crumbs add just the right amount of texture and crunch.

Serves 4

350g (12oz) dried or tinned white beans (haricot or navy)

1 bay leaf

1 fresh thyme sprig

Salt and freshly ground white pepper

4 very large firm red tomatoes

125ml (4fl oz) extra-virgin olive oil

8 rashers bacon

20 garlic cloves, peeled

225g (8oz) potatoes, peeled and finely chopped

225g (8oz) white onions, finely chopped

350ml (12fl oz) *Vodka Chicken Broth* (see page 126), *Vodka Beef Broth* (see page 127) or stock

1 tablespoon *Basil Vodka* (see page 146) or 2 tablespoons freshly chopped basil

125ml (4fl oz) vodka

4 tablespoons cream

1 Soak the dried beans in cold water for 8–10 hours. Drain and rinse. If using tinned beans, drain and rinse before cooking.

2 Place the beans in a medium saucepan with enough water to cover by about 5cm (2in). Add the bay leaf and thyme and bring to the boil. Reduce the heat, cover and cook until the beans are tender – about 1 hour. Add 1 teaspoon salt and ½ teaspoon white pepper. Strain, remove and discard the bay leaf and thyme, and set aside.

3 Carefully cut off the tops of the tomatoes and hollow out to create a bowl (be sure not to make any holes in the sides or bottom of the tomatoes). Set aside.

4 Preheat the oven to 170°C/325°F/gas mark 3.

5 Heat 1 tablespoon of the olive oil in a large frying pan over a high heat and fry the bacon until crisp. Transfer the bacon to kitchen paper to drain any excess grease. Then chop the rashers finely and set aside.

6 Place the garlic in a small baking dish with a little of the remaining olive oil, cover with aluminium foil and bake until golden brown – about 35 minutes.

7 Meanwhile, add the potatoes and onions with the rest of the oil to the pan used to fry the bacon, reduce the heat to moderate and cook until tender – about 6–8 minutes. Add a pinch of salt and pepper and set aside.

8 Put the garlic (with any remaining oil), the potato/onion mixture and beans in a blender or food-processor with the broth, *Basil Vodka* and vodka and pulse until smooth.

9 Warm in a medium saucepan over moderate heat for 10 minutes or until hot. Swirl in the cream and season to taste with salt and white pepper.

10 Meanwhile place the tomatoes, cut-side down, on a baking sheet or in a roasting tin and roast for about 5–7 minutes, checking frequently as the tomatoes must remain firm.

11 To assemble, place each tomato in the centre of a shallow bowl or soup plate. Fill the tomato with the soup and crumble chopped bacon over the top.

PLUCKY PUMPKIN SOUP WITH CINNAMON CROÛTONS

This is my favourite autumn soup. Vodka seems to accentuate the pumpkin flavour and the cinnamon croûtons are a sweet addition that elevates this soup from simple to sublime. (Don't panic. I didn't know croûtons could do that either.)

Serves 4–6

25g (1oz) butter

225g (8oz) onions, chopped

1 rasher bacon, chopped

4 tablespoons vodka

900kg (2lb) fresh pumpkin, peeled, seeded and chopped

1 tablespoon very finely chopped fresh ginger

1 teaspoon salt

450ml (16fl oz) *Vodka Chicken Broth* (see page 126)

1 teaspoon brown sugar

¼ teaspoon ground cinnamon

⅛ teaspoon freshly ground white pepper

125ml (4fl oz) double cream

Cinnamon Croûtons (see recipe below)

1 tablespoon grated nutmeg

1 Melt the butter in a heavy-bottomed saucepan over a moderate heat and add the onions and bacon. Cook until the onions are soft – about 5 minutes.

2 Stir in the vodka to deglaze the pan, followed immediately by the pumpkin, ginger and salt, and cook until the pumpkin is soft – about 15 minutes.

3 Add the *Vodka Chicken Broth*, sugar, cinnamon and white pepper, increase the heat to high and bring to the boil. Cook for about 2 minutes, stirring frequently. Reduce the heat to low and simmer for about 15 minutes.

4 Remove from the heat, place in a blender or food-processor and whizz to a smooth purée.

5 Return the soup mixture to the pan, cover, bring to the boil and cook for about 3 minutes. Reduce the heat to low, stir in the cream and simmer on low until ready to serve, stirring occasionally.

6 Serve in bowls topped with cinnamon croûtons and dusted with nutmeg.

CINNAMON CROÛTONS

40g (1½oz) butter, softened

1 tablespoon brown sugar

¼ teaspoon ground cinnamon

4 slices white or wholewheat bread

1 Preheat the oven to 200°C/400°F/gas mark 6.

2 Combine the butter, brown sugar and cinnamon. Spread the mixture evenly over one side of each bread slice.

3 Place the bread, buttered-side up, on a baking tray and bake until crisp – about 8–10 minutes.

4 Cut each slice of bread into small triangles or squares.

At Hallowe'en, you might cut the bread into shapes that represent the eyes, nose and mouth of a jack-o'-lantern and set them in appropriate places in the centre of Plucky Pumpkin Soup. It's a little hokey, perhaps. But, then, so am I.

CHILLED TOMATO CITRUS VODKA SOUP WITH FRIED APPLE RINGS

I'm a big fan of the sweet and savoury combination in this cool summer soup. (But I guess that's obvious since I've gone to all the trouble of putting it in this book.)

Serves 6

2 apples, cored and sliced into thin rings

125ml (4fl oz) vegetable oil

2 tablespoons extra-virgin olive oil

10 medium plum tomatoes, seeded and finely chopped

110g (4oz) shallots, chopped

1 tablespoon very finely chopped fresh ginger

1 tablespoon chopped garlic

2 tablespoons honey

450ml (16fl oz) *Vodka Chicken Broth* (see page 126) or chicken stock

225ml (8fl oz) dry white wine

125ml (4fl oz) freshly squeezed lime juice

4 tablespoons freshly chopped coriander

2 tablespoons freshly chopped mint

2 teaspoons grated lime zest

2 tablespoons freshly squeezed lemon juice

4 tablespoons vodka

Salt and freshly ground pepper

Ground cinnamon (optional)

1 Pat the apple rings dry between layers of kitchen paper.

2 Heat the vegetable oil in a large deep-sided frying pan over a high heat and fry the apples in small batches, stirring, for 1–2 minutes or until they are crisp.

3 Transfer the fried apples with a slotted spoon to kitchen paper to drain off the excess oil and set aside.

4 Heat the olive oil in a large saucepan over a moderate heat. Add the tomatoes, shallots, ginger and garlic. Simmer until the liquid evaporates and the mixture thickens – about 12 minutes.

5 Add the honey and simmer until the mixture is very thick, stirring frequently – about 8 minutes.

6 Add the *Vodka Chicken Broth*, wine, lime juice, coriander, mint and lime zest and simmer for about 30 minutes.

7 Pass the soup through a sieve into large bowl, pressing on the solids to release the juices. Discard the solids.

8 Stir the lemon juice and vodka into soup and season with salt and pepper to taste. Chill for at least 8 hours.

9 Serve in large bowls garnished with the fried apple rings. Dust with cinnamon if desired.

Let's talk turkey… and chicken and duck. In this chapter you'll learn to use vodka marinades and brines to infuse poultry with flavour and keep the flesh moist – even when subjected to scorching heat and long cooking times. Sure, it takes more patience and planning to produce some of these dishes. But it's well worth it if you never want to taste desiccated roast chicken or turkey again.

Of course, if you are short on time, you'll also discover how quickly vodka sauces and glazes can add unique and intense flavours. You will even find out how the vodka bottle itself can become a cooking apparatus. Now doesn't that sound like fun?

POULTRY

CHICKEN ON THE BOTTLE
(with Basil Potatoes)

This recipe uses a bottle of vodka. An empty bottle of vodka (how you empty it is up to you). I guess you could use any bottle for this recipe. But, in case you hadn't noticed, I've got a theme goin' here! Just pick a bottle big enough to support the chicken.

Fact is, Russians have been using bottles to roast chickens for as far back as anyone can remember. Combined with my vodka brine, this method results in a moist bird with crispy skin. And it allows much of the fat to drain off. Of course, you can use a roasting rack instead of a bottle if you prefer. The vodka brine will still work its magic.

Serves 6

1 whole roasting chicken, about 2–3kg
   (4½–6½lb), after vodka brining
   (see instructions on page 64)
1 vodka bottle, empty
4 tablespoons butter
1 tablespoon vodka
1 tablespoon honey
1 teaspoon dry mustard
Salt
2 tablespoons olive oil
450g (1lb) potatoes, scrubbed and
   quartered
1 onion, thinly sliced
1 red pepper, de-seeded and sliced
2 tablespoons freshly chopped basil
2 tablespoons chopped garlic
Coarse sea salt and freshly ground black
   pepper

1 Follow the instructions on page 64 for *Vodka Brine for Chicken and Turkey*.
2 Take an empty ovenproof bottle. Half-fill the bottle with water and place the open bottle upright in the centre of a medium roasting tin.
3 Preheat the oven to 220°C/425°F/gas mark 7 and adjust the shelf so that when placed on the bottle, the chicken sits at about the centre of the oven (in smaller ovens you may have to remove all the shelves and set the tin at the bottom of the oven).
4 Remove the bottle from the oven and, to put it politely, 'sit' the chicken on the bottle so that the bottle pokes up through the chicken's neck. (You may insert a meat thermometer into the thickest part of the chicken at this point, but it should not touch the bone.)
5 Melt the butter in the microwave with vodka, honey, mustard and ½ teaspoon of salt.
6 Brush the chicken with the butter mixture and roast until the skin is golden brown and crispy – about 25–30 minutes.
7 Reduce the oven temperature to 180°C/350°F/gas mark 4 and continue to roast the chicken until cooked through – when the legs move freely and the juices run clear when poked with a fork, or until the thermometer reads 82°C (180°F). Remove the chicken from the oven and leave to rest, covered, in a warm place.
8 Meanwhile, to prepare the basil potatoes, heat the olive oil in a large heavy-bottomed frying pan over a moderate heat and sauté the potatoes, onion, red pepper, basil and chopped garlic until the potatoes are well browned and cooked through. Add coarse sea salt and pepper to taste.
9 When ready, remove the chicken from the bottle, carve into portions and serve with the basil potatoes.

GLAZED AND CONFUSED CHICKEN
(Grilled Chicken with Vodka Apricot and Cumin Glaze)

The combination of sweet Vodka Apricot Date Jam and cumin results in a very distinctive glaze for this grilled chicken dish. Have plenty of bread on hand and, when no one is looking, use it to mop up the extra sauce on your plate. Yes, it's that good.

Serves 4

4 boneless, skinless chicken breasts, rinsed and patted dry

Salt and freshly ground black pepper, to taste

1 tablespoon freshly squeezed lemon juice

2 tablespoons extra-virgin olive oil

2 tablespoons finely chopped shallots

1 teaspoon crushed garlic (about 2 cloves)

4 tablespoons vodka

175g (6oz) *Vodka Apricot Date Jam* (see page 135), or apricot jam

½ teaspoon ground cumin

⅛ teaspoon cayenne pepper

1 fresh apricot, sliced, to garnish

Plain steamed rice, to serve

1 Preheat the oven to 150°C/300°F/gas mark 2.

2 Heat a griddle pan on a high heat for 6–8 minutes.

3 Trim chicken breasts and season with salt, pepper and lemon juice and 1 tablespoon of the oil.

4 Quickly sear the chicken on the griddle pan – about 1 minute each side (remember to the rotate chicken 90° every 30 seconds to create a cross-hatch of grill marks). Then transfer to an ovenproof dish and set aside.

5 Put the remaining oil in a medium saucepan over a moderate-high heat, and sauté the shallots with the garlic until soft – about 3 minutes. Add the vodka, then the jam, cumin, cayenne pepper and salt and pepper to taste. Bring to the boil and cook for 2–3 minutes.

6 Immediately pour the glaze over the chicken to cover and place the baking dish in the oven. Bake until the chicken is cooked through – about 10–20 minutes depending on the size of the breasts.

7 Flip the chicken a few times in the glaze to coat thoroughly and serve each breast atop a scoop of steamed rice. Garnish with the slices of apricot.

It is very easy to overcook chicken breasts. Moist and juicy at 71°C (160°F); tough and dry at any temperature over 74°C (165°F). If you don't use a meat thermometer, cook the chicken until the meat releases clear, not pink, juices when pricked with a fork or knife.

VODKA BRINE FOR CHICKEN AND TURKEY

I prefer to introduce flavour into meat and poultry before cooking. Brining is the process of submerging meats or poultry in a solution that contains salt and other ingredients that will tenderise, add flavour and ensure moisture prior to roasting. While most recipes call for seasoning to the surface of the flesh, brining allows the seasonings actually to penetrate and permeate the meat – in this case, intensified by the vodka. This pre-treatment produces a wonderfully moist and well-seasoned bird.

It's best if the bird is submerged in brine for 6–8 hours (longer if it has been frozen) and then left to dry in the fridge overnight (or for a minimum of 8–10 hours) before cooking. The skin must be totally dry or the meat will steam in the oven. The drier the skin, the better it will crisp while cooking.

4–8 litres (1–2 gallons) ice-cold water – enough to cover the bird

225ml (8fl oz) vodka

450g (1lb) coarse salt

225g (8oz) granulated sugar

2 tablespoons freshly ground black pepper

1 tablespoon dried thyme

1 tablespoon oregano

3 bay leaves

1 Mix all the ingredients in a large bucket, pan or cooler until they are completely dissolved. Put the container in the fridge or a very cool spot. Add ice packs (ice in sealed plastic bags will do) to keep the contents at or below about 5°C (40°F) during the entire brining process.

2 Wash the bird inside and out and remove the neck (as well as the giblets and tail pieces on turkeys).

3 Immerse the bird, breast-side down, in the brine and soak for 6–8 hours – weighing it down with a heavy object (like a plastic container filled with water) to keep it completely immersed. Replace the ice packs if necessary to maintain the temperature.

4 Remove the bird from the brine and rinse inside and out under cold running water. Pat dry inside and out with kitchen paper and place in a shallow pan or container in your fridge for at least 3 hours or overnight. (This allows the skin to dry out so it becomes crisp during roasting.)

Table salt (rather than kosher salt or coarse sea salt) can be used to make the brine. However, kosher salt is recommended since table salt contains anti-caking ingredients, iodine and other additives.

VODKA HASH AND HOT BISCUITS

Hash was invented to use up the remains of a feast, so this recipe calls for leftover roasted chicken or turkey meat. If you would like to cook this dish from scratch, just season 2–3 chicken or turkey breasts with salt and freshly ground black pepper, drizzle with oil and roast in the oven until browned and cooked through. Then chop and begin this recipe.

Serves 4–6

1 tablespoon extra-virgin olive oil

60g (2½oz) bacon, chopped

350g (12oz) onion, thinly sliced

40g (1½oz) celery, finely chopped

75ml (3fl oz) vodka

450g (1lb) chicken or turkey, roasted and chopped

1 tablespoon *KGB Sauce* (see page 124), or hot red pepper sauce

25g (1oz) butter

3 tablespoons flour

50ml (2fl oz) single cream

Salt and freshly ground black pepper

Hot Biscuits, to serve (see recipe below)

1 Heat the oil in a medium frying pan over a high heat and cook the bacon for about 2 minutes. Add the onions and celery and cook until soft – about 5 minutes. Deglaze the pan by adding the vodka and stirring.

2 Toss the chicken or turkey with KGB Sauce in a small bowl and then add to pan. Cook for about 5 minutes and remove from the heat.

3 Meanwhile, make a *roux* by melting the butter in a small saucepan over a moderate heat, whisking in the flour and cooking it until it becomes lightly browned and has a nutty aroma – about 5 minutes. Stir in the cream and add salt and pepper to taste.

4 Pour the sauce over the chicken, return the pan to the heat and simmer for about 15 minutes. Serve with *Hot Biscuits* and butter (see recipe below).

HOT BISCUITS

No vodka here – but it is an ideal and relatively quick accompaniment to the Vodka Hash described above.

Makes 10–12

200g (14oz) flour

1 tablespoon baking powder

2 teaspoons salt

175ml (6fl oz) single cream

2 eggs, beaten

1 Preheat the oven to 180°C/350°F/gas mark 4.

2 Sift together the flour, baking powder and salt into a medium mixing bowl.

3 In a separate bowl, beat the cream with the eggs and then stir into the flour with a wooden spoon. Do not over-mix. The batter should be soft and lumpy.

4 Heap tablespoonfuls of the batter on to a greased baking sheet. Bake until golden brown – about 10 minutes – and serve immediately with butter.

VODKA LEMON CHICKEN

Lemon chicken is among the most common recipes for preparing chicken breasts. Here's my uncommon vodka variation.

Serves 2–4

1 lemon, thinly sliced

2 tablespoons extra-virgin olive oil

2 eggs

2 tablespoons milk

75g (3oz) flour

4 large boneless, skinless chicken
    breasts, rinsed and patted dry

4 tablespoons vodka

50g (2oz) unsalted butter

4 tablespoons fresh lemon juice

½ tablespoon freshly chopped parsley

1 tablespoon freshly chopped basil

4 tablespoons capers

Salt and freshly ground black pepper

1 Quickly char the lemon slices on both sides in a medium sauté pan over a high heat and set aside. Return the pan to a moderate heat and add the oil.
2 Beat the eggs and milk in a small shallow bowl. Tip the flour into another shallow bowl. Dredge a chicken breast in the flour, and then in the egg mixture. Place immediately in the pan. Repeat with the remaining breasts and sauté the chicken until golden and cooked through – approximately 5–7 minutes on each side (depending on their size). Set aside in a covered dish.
3 Deglaze the pan with the vodka and loosen the flavour bits at the bottom of the pan by scraping with a wooden spoon. Then add the butter, lemon juice, parsley, basil, capers, salt and pepper. Continue to cook until the mixture reduces by about a quarter. Return the chicken and grilled lemon slices to the pan and toss.
4 Serve the chicken breasts topped with the sauce. Boiled linguine mixed with a little of the lemon sauce makes a fine side dish.

SAUCED CHICKEN

(Chicken in Vodka Orange Cream Sauce)

A sauced and saucy bird.

Serves 4

1 tablespoon extra-virgin olive oil

2 tablespoons finely chopped red onion

4 tablespoons *Orange Peel Vodka* (see
    page 142)

2 tablespoons *Lemon Peel Vodka* (see
    page 142)

125ml (4fl oz) fresh orange juice

225ml (8fl oz) *Vodka Chicken Broth* (see
    page 126)

4 tablespoons double cream

Salt and freshly ground black pepper

4 boneless, skinless chicken breasts,
    rinsed and patted dry

1 Preheat the oven to 190°C/375°F/gas mark 5.
2 Heat the olive oil in a small saucepan over a moderate heat. Add the red onion and sauté for about 2–3 minutes.
3 Add both the vodkas, the orange juice and *Vodka Chicken Broth* and bring to the boil.
4 Immediately reduce the heat and add the cream, stirring constantly until the sauce thickens – about 4–5 minutes. Add salt and pepper to taste; set aside and keep warm.
5 Place the chicken breasts in a greased baking dish, lightly season with salt and pepper and cook in the oven for 35–40 minutes.
6 During the last 15 minutes of cooking, pour about half the sauce over the chicken.
7 Serve the chicken with the remaining sauce and steamed vegetables.

CHICKEN KIEV WITH VODKA CREAMED CORN

Chicken Kiev is served at many formal dinners in Russia. Somehow caterers at these events prepare the dish in such a way as to guarantee that molten butter squirts from the centre of the chicken and on to my tie. But that didn't stop me from trying my hand at creating my version of this classic dish.

Serves 4

4 boneless, skinless chicken breasts, rinsed and patted dry
225ml (8fl oz) buttermilk
1 teaspoon coarse salt
1 teaspoon freshly ground black pepper
40g (1½oz) unsalted butter
2 tablespoons finely chopped spring onions
2 tablespoons finely chopped fresh parsley
2 eggs, beaten
3 tablespoons vodka
75g (3oz) flour
75g (3oz) breadcrumbs, seasoned with salt and freshly ground black pepper
Vodka Creamed Corn (see recipe below)

1 Trim the chicken breasts and pound with the flat side of a chef's knife or meat tenderiser to 3mm (⅛in) thick.

2 Soak the chicken breasts in the buttermilk, salt and pepper in a covered bowl or a re-sealable plastic bag and refrigerate for at least 2 hours.

3 Pat the chicken dry and discard the marinade. Cut the butter into quarters and lay one piece in the centre of each chicken breast. Evenly distribute the spring onions and parsley over each breast.

4 Roll the breasts to contain the ingredients and secure with cocktail sticks (counting how many you use so you can retrieve them all before serving).

5 Mix the eggs and vodka in a small shallow bowl. Tip the flour and bread-crumbs into two bowls. Roll the breasts in flour, then dip in egg and roll in breadcrumbs. Wrap in cling film and refrigerate for 1 hour or overnight.

6 Preheat the oven to 190°C/375°F/gas mark 5.

7 Heat the oil in a large heavy-bottomed frying pan over a moderate-high heat. Cook the chicken until golden on all sides – about 5 minutes. Transfer to kitchen paper to absorb the excess oil.

8 Transfer the chicken to a baking tray. Cover with aluminium foil and bake until cooked through – about 20–25 minutes. Remove the cocktail sticks and serve hot with the *Vodka Creamed Corn*.

VODKA CREAMED CORN

Creamed corn was a staple of my childhood. But this is better (sorry, Mom). When fresh sweetcorn is in season, I grill the cobs lightly and cut the kernels from them – this adds a slightly smoky flavour.

Serves 4–6

75g (3oz) unsalted butter
900g (2lb) sweetcorn kernels, fresh, tinned or frozen
150ml (¼ pint) single cream
150ml (¼ pint) *Vodka Chicken Broth* (see page 126)
1 tablespoon cornflour
1 teaspoon sugar
3 tablespoons vodka
1 teaspoon *Vanilla Vodka* (see page 143) or vanilla extract

1 Melt the butter in a large frying pan over a moderate heat. Stir in the sweetcorn, followed by the cream, *Vodka Chicken Broth*, cornflour, sugar and vodka. Cook, stirring constantly, until the mixture thickens – 5–6 minutes.

2 Add the *Vanilla Vodka* and salt and pepper to taste. Serve garnished with fresh parsley or chopped spring onions.

DISORIENTED DUCK
(Grilled Duck Breast with Vodka Cranberry Orange Glaze)

Why is this bird disoriented? Could be that nasty 'quack' habit. But in spite of the whimsical name, this is a serious dish that couldn't be easier to prepare – or more flavourful.

Serves 4

225g (8oz) whole cranberries, fresh or frozen

125ml (4fl oz) *Orange Peel Vodka* (see page 142) or vodka

225ml (8fl oz) orange marmalade

2 large duck breasts, skin on

Salt and freshly ground black pepper, to taste

Basil Potatoes (see page 62) or roast potatoes and steamed asparagus or broccoli to serve

1 Combine the cranberries, *Orange Peel Vodka* and marmalade in a medium saucepan and bring to the boil. Reduce the heat and simmer, stirring occasionally, until it becomes thick – about 10 minutes. Cover and keep warm.

2 Wash the duck breasts thoroughly under cold running water, pat dry and place them, skin-side down, on a clean cutting board. Cut each breast in half down the centre to create 4 pieces. Then trim away any fat that visibly extends past the edges of the exposed meat – leaving the layer of fat on one side. Season with salt and pepper.

3 Preheat a griddle pan over a high heat and griddle the breast pieces, fat-side down until the fat has rendered off and the skin is golden brown – about 8–10 minutes. Turn the breasts over, baste with the sauce and cook to desired doneness – about 5 more minutes for medium-rare. Remove the duck from the pan, loosely cover with aluminium foil and leave it to rest for 2–3 minutes (which allows the natural juices to redistribute throughout the meat).

4 Slice the breasts thinly, cutting against the grain, and fan the pieces out on 4 warm plates. Spoon the sauce over the top. Serve with *Basil Potatoes* or roast potatoes and steamed asparagus or broccoli.

Using the same brining recipe recommended for Chicken on the Bottle (see page 62), this turkey dinner is time-consuming, but well worth it for a holiday or special occasion. I prefer to cook the stuffing separately – rather than inside the bird – because it's difficult to coordinate the cooking of the stuffing with that of the turkey. And I'm lazy.

Serves 6–8

1 turkey, about 5.5–6.4kg (12–14lb)

50g (2oz) butter, softened

4 tablespoons chopped shallots

1 tablespoon plain flour

4 tablespoons vodka

125ml (4fl oz) *Vodka Chicken Broth* (see page 126)

Salt and freshly ground black pepper, to taste

1 Brine the turkey following the instructions on page 64.

2 Preheat the oven to 200°C/400°F/gas mark 6.

3 Set the turkey, breast-side down, in a heavy-duty V-rack on a shallow roasting tin. Tie the legs together and tuck the wings underneath the bird. Coat the skin with the butter.

4 Roast the turkey for 1 hour, then lower the temperature to 130°C/250°F/gas mark ½ and roast for a further 1½–2 hours – or, if you have a meat thermometer, until the breast temperature reaches 63–66°C (145–150°F).

5 Remove the turkey from the oven (close the oven door), flip the turkey breast-side up, baste and return to the oven.

6 Raise the oven temperature again to 200°C/400°F/gas mark 6 and cook until the temperature in the thickest part of the thigh reaches 82°C (180°F) or the thigh juices run clear when pierced with a fork – about 2½–3 hours.

7 Remove the turkey from the oven and let it rest for about 15–20 minutes before carving to allow the juices to saturate the meat evenly.

8 To make the *Vodka Pan Gravy*, set the roasting tin on the hob over a moderate-high heat, add the shallots and cook until soft – about 4 minutes. Whisk in the flour and continue to cook for another 2–3 minutes. Deglaze the tin by adding the vodka and use the whisk to scrape any lingering food bits from the bottom of the tin. Add the *Vodka Chicken Broth* and bring to the boil. Strain into a bowl and add salt and pepper to taste.

9 Serve with the gravy, *Vodka Fruit & Nut Stuffing* and *Apple Cranberry Vodka Relish*.

(Roast Turkey with Vodka Pan Gravy, Vodka Fruit & Nut Stuffing and Apple Cranberry Vodka Relish)

TIPSY TURKEY

VODKA FRUIT & NUT STUFFING

If you believe better stuffings have more stuff, this recipe should serve you well.

Serves 6–8

175g (6oz) whole fresh or frozen and defrosted blackcurrants
125ml (4fl oz) *Apple Vodka* (see page 143)
110g (4oz) wild rice
350ml (12fl oz) freshly squeezed orange juice
225g (8oz) long-grain white or brown rice
600ml (1 pint) *Vodka Chicken Broth* (see page 126)
350g (12oz) cooking apples, peeled, cored and finely chopped
450g (1lb) onions, finely chopped
225g (8oz) celery, finely chopped
4 tablespoons olive oil
110g (4oz) dried cranberries
20 dried apricot halves
225g (8oz) sultanas
110g (4oz) cashew nuts, chopped
75g (3oz) pine kernels
1 teaspoon dried thyme or wild sage
Salt and freshly ground black pepper, to taste

1 Soak the blackcurrants in the *Apple Vodka* for about 1 hour.
2 Cook the wild rice in a small saucepan with the orange juice over a moderate heat until tender – about 10 minutes. Set aside, but do not drain.
3 Cook the long-grain rice in a small pot with the *Vodka Chicken Broth* over a moderate heat until tender – about 10 minutes. Set aside, but do not drain.
4 Cook the apples, onions and celery with the olive oil in a large pot over a moderate heat, stirring frequently, for about 10 minutes. Reduce the heat to a simmer.
5 Stir in the blackcurrants with the vodka, wild rice with orange juice and long-grain rice with broth.
6 Stir in the remaining ingredients, season with salt and pepper and simmer, covered, for about 30 minutes, or until needed.

APPLE CRANBERRY VODKA RELISH

I can no longer imagine turkey without this cranberry concoction to accompany it.

Serves 6–8

175g (6oz) fresh or frozen and defrosted cranberries
175g (6oz) currants
1.3kg (3lb) dessert apples, peeled, cored and finely chopped
4 tablespoons light brown sugar
4 tablespoons *Apple Vodka* (see page 143)

1 Using a potato masher, crush the cranberries in a large saucepan. Add 125ml (4fl oz) water and the currants. Let stand for about 20 minutes.
2 Cook the mixture, covered, over a moderate heat for about 5 minutes. Stir in the apples. Cook, covered, over a low heat, for about 5–7 minutes.
3 Raise the heat to moderate-high, add the sugar and cook until the apples are very soft – about 10 minutes. Remove from the heat.
4 Add the *Apple Vodka* and mash the apple and cranberry mixture again. Stir and serve warm.

DINNER

Vodka has a magical effect on meats. The vodka helps to break down fibres to tenderise the cut while infusing marinades and spices into the meat. It also helps to intensify sauces used to enhance the enjoyment of fresh cuts of beef. And sometimes, vodka is used to deglaze a pan and reclaim the wonderful flavour from bits seared to its bottom (which may sound painful, but is really an important flavour step).

Of course, all this preparation and innovation will be wasted on a poor cut of beef. Unfortunately, many supermarket meats toughen easily and are sadly lacking in flavour. So my advice is to befriend (bribe) a reliable butcher and demand quality in every cut.

SHASHLIK DRENCHED IN POMEGRANATE AND VODKA

Maybe you call it barbecue or shish kebab. But in Russia it's called shashlik (pronounced 'shash-leek'). And it's a summer staple when many Muscovites escape the heat and smog to their 'dachas' on the outskirts of the metropolis.

Serves 8

1.3kg (3lb) pork loin or lamb, trimmed of excess fat and cut into 5cm (2in) chunks

450ml (16fl oz) pomegranate juice

225ml (8fl oz) *Lemon Peel Vodka* (see page 142)

225g (8oz) onions, chopped

2 tablespoons chopped fresh parsley

2 tablespoons *KGB Sauce* (see page 124) or hot red pepper sauce

1 tablespoon crushed garlic

1 tablespoon coarse sea salt

1 teaspoon freshly ground black pepper

3 onions, quartered

3 red or green peppers, de-seeded and quartered

3 tomatoes, quartered

4 tablespoons canola or grapeseed oil

4 heavy skewers, approximately 40cm (15in)

1 Place the meat in a large re-sealable plastic bag with the pomegranate juice, vodka, chopped onions, parsley, *KGB Sauce*, garlic, salt and pepper. Refrigerate for about 6 hours or overnight, turning occasionally.

2 Remove the meat from the marinade and pat dry (reserving the marinade). Skewer the meat, alternating with the quartered onions, peppers and tomatoes. The pieces should be tightly packed together.

3 Preheat a griddle pan or grill until hot. Brush the shashlik with oil and cook, turning often, until the meat is seared and cooked to your liking – about 15–20 minutes. Allow the meat to rest on the skewers for about 2–3 minutes before serving.

4 Meanwhile, bring the reserved marinade to the boil in a medium saucepan and cook for about 2–3 minutes. Reduce to a simmer and continue to cook until it is reduced by approximately a third – about 15 minutes. Strain the sauce and pour into a dipping bowl.

5 Remove the meat and vegetables from the skewers and serve with the dipping sauce.

MOSCOW TACOS

I think it was my ol' pal Jon Stetson who once quipped (or maybe it was those voices in my head again) that all Mexican food is the same – just folded differently. Lay it flat, it's a tostada. Fold it and it becomes a taco. Roll it up and it's an enchilada. You get the idea. Anyway, here's how I make a Mexican meal – Moscow style.

Serves 6

450g (1lb) dried pinto beans

2 tablespoons olive oil

1 large onion, finely chopped

450g (1lb) minced beef

3 tablespoons vodka

Salt and freshly ground black pepper

800ml (28 fl oz) *Vodka Chicken Broth* (see page 126)

1 tablespoon *KGB Sauce* (see page 124) or hot pepper sauce

1 tablespoon freshly squeezed lemon juice

2 garlic cloves, crushed

2 teaspoons ground cumin

2 teaspoons dried oregano or 4 tablespoons chopped fresh oregano

2 teaspoons dried basil or 4 tablespoons chopped fresh basil

6 large tortillas or *Moscow Fry Bread* (see page 128)

2 large tomatoes, sliced

600g (1¼lb) cheddar cheese, grated

450g (1lb) lettuce, shredded

110g (4oz) jalapeño chillies, chopped

225ml (8fl oz) *Roasted Pepper Salsa à la Vodka* (see page 129) or your favourite taco salsa

225ml (8fl oz) sour cream (optional)

1 Soak the beans in cold water for 8–10 hours. Drain and rinse.

2 Put the beans into a large saucepan with enough fresh water to cover them by 2.5cm (1in). Simmer over a low heat until the beans are barely tender – approximately 2 hours. Drain and cool.

3 Heat 1 tablespoon of the olive oil in large saucepan over a moderate heat. Add the onion and cook, stirring often, until soft – about 5 minutes. Reduce the heat to a simmer and add the beans to the onion.

4 Heat the remaining olive oil in a large sauté pan, crumble in the minced beef and cook over a high heat until well browned. Stir in the vodka and a pinch of salt and pepper. Add to the beans and onion.

5 Stir in the *Vodka Chicken Broth*, *KGB Sauce*, lemon juice, garlic, cumin, oregano and basil. Bring to the boil, then reduce the heat and simmer until the mixture becomes thick. Add salt and pepper to taste.

6 Spoon the beef mixture on to the tortillas or *Moscow Fry Bread*, top with the remaining ingredients and serve with *Vodka Black Bean And Grilled Sweetcorn Salad* (see page 51).

ROAST PORK LOIN WITH VODKA MUSTARD GRAVY AND APPLE VODKA SWEET POTATOES

Start with a great pork loin, present it as described and you cannot fail to impress with this dish. The Apple Vodka marinade acts much like a brine to infuse the meat with flavour and moisture.

Serves 6–8

900g (2lb) boneless pork loin

225ml (8fl oz) *Apple Vodka* (see page 143)

225g (8oz) onions, thinly sliced

1 tablespoon crushed garlic

2 tablespoons coarse sea salt

1 teaspoon freshly ground black pepper

1 tablespoon *KGB Sauce* (see page 124), or hot red pepper sauce

2 tablespoons canola or grapeseed oil

4 rashers bacon

Apple Sweet Vodka Potatoes (see recipe right)

1 tablespoon plain flour

450ml (16fl oz) *Vodka Chicken Broth* (see page 126) or chicken stock

110g (4oz) wholegrain mustard

1 apple, thinly sliced, to garnish

1 Rinse and pat dry the pork and place in a re-sealable plastic bag with the *Apple Vodka*, onions, garlic, salt, black pepper and *KGB Sauce* for 8–24 hours.

2 Preheat the oven to 180°C/350°F/gas mark 4.

3 Heat the oil in a large heavy-based roasting tin over a high heat.

4 Remove the pork from the bag (reserving the marinade), pat dry and sear in the roasting tin, turning frequently till browned evenly on all sides – about 5 minutes.

5 Remove the tin from the heat, drape the bacon rashers over the pork and place the tin on the centre shelf of the oven. Cook as desired – about 25–30 minutes for medium doneness.

6 Prepare the *Apple Vodka Sweet Potatoes* (recipe right) and keep warm.

7 Remove the tin from the oven, transfer the pork to a carving surface (ideally on a rack that allows the juices to run off) and let rest. Reserve the fat in the tin.

8 Return the roasting tin to the hob over a moderate heat, add the reserved marinade and fat and cook until the onions become translucent – about 5 minutes.

9 Whisk in the flour, *Vodka Chicken Broth* and mustard and continue stirring, incorporating any scrapings from the bottom of the tin, while you slowly bring the mixture to a simmer for about 5 minutes.

10 Pass the mixture through a sieve into a small bowl and add salt and pepper to taste.

11 To serve, place a large scoop of *Apple Vodka Sweet Potatoes* in the centre of a warmed plate and insert a large apple slice (upright) into the centre of the potatoes. Slice the pork and lay 2–3 slices on the potatoes around the apple slice. Spoon some gravy on top of each slice.

APPLE VODKA SWEET POTATOES

This sweet mash is the ideal complement to any pork dish.

Serves 6–8

1.3kg (3lb) sweet potatoes, peeled and chopped

Salt and freshly ground black pepper

25g (1oz) butter

110g (4oz) onions, finely chopped

700g (1½lb) apples, peeled and finely chopped

4 tablespoons brown sugar

4 tablespoons *Apple Vodka* (see page 143)

1 Boil the sweet potatoes in a large saucepan of water with 1 tablespoon of salt until soft – about 8–10 minutes. Drain and mash.

2 Melt the butter in a large sauté pan over a moderate heat until it begins to brown. Add the onions and apples and cook until the apples are very soft – about 5–7 minutes.

3 Add the brown sugar and cook until the sugar completely dissolves – about 2 minutes.

4 Deglaze the pan by adding the *Apple Vodka* and cook until the mixture begins to thicken – about 1 minute. Add the apple mixture to the sweet potatoes. Mix thoroughly, add salt and pepper to taste and serve.

GRILLED FILET MIGNON AND PRAWNS WITH VODKA TERIYAKI SAUCE

Japanese-born chef Tom Kurokawa is a fourth-generation restaurateur who has operated several restaurants in Japan and New York. Lucky for me (and you) he was also an eager contributor to this book. This dish is a confluence of Tom's fusion-style cuisine with our favourite ingredient. Goodbye sake. Hello vodka.

Serves 4

Vodka Teriyaki Sauce (see recipe below), warmed

4 thick filet mignon steaks, at room temperature

Coarse sea salt and freshly ground black pepper

10g (½oz) butter

2 tablespoons canola or grapeseed oil

20 large prawns, peeled and de-veined

Mixed herbs (such as basil, chives, chervil, parsley, tarragon)

1 Preheat the oven to 200°C/400°F/gas mark 6.

2 Prepare the *Vodka Teriyaki Sauce* and keep warm.

3 Generously season the steaks with salt and pepper.

4 Heat the butter and oil in a large ovenproof frying pan over a moderate heat. When the butter melts, add the steaks, increase the heat to high and sear for about 3 minutes on each side. Reduce the heat to moderate and cook to the desired doneness – about 8 minutes total for medium-rare. Remove the steaks from the pan and allow to rest.

5 Add the prawns to the same pan and put in the oven to cook until pink and firm – about 3–5 minutes depending on their size.

6 Meanwhile, chop all the herbs into large bite-size pieces and pile on to the centres of warmed plates.

7 To serve, place a steak over the herbs on each plate and top with the prawns and about 2 tablespoons *Vodka Teriyaki Sauce.*

Chef Tom serves this dish with wasabi-mashed potatoes – which you can easily prepare at home using wasabi powder, a ground, dried horseradish available at most grocers. Simply follow the instructions on the pack for mixing it into a paste and add it to your favourite mashed potato recipe.

VODKA TERIYAKI SAUCE

Chef Tom perfected his vodka version of this classic Japanese sauce at his Moscow Crab House kitchen. It can be used as a marinade or to brush over meat, chicken, fish or vegetables when grilling, or as a dipping sauce.

225ml (8fl oz) vodka

225g (8oz) brown sugar

225ml (8fl oz) soy sauce

225ml (8fl oz) *Vodka Chicken Broth* (see page 126) or chicken stock

1 garlic clove

1 slice fresh ginger

1 bay leaf

1 ancho chilli or Mexican sweet chilli

1 *Over-heated Tomato* (see page 33) or sun-dried tomato

1 Put all the ingredients in a large saucepan and simmer over a moderate heat until reduced by half – about 45 minutes.

2 Pass through a fine sieve.

3 Cool, then store in the fridge until needed. The sauce will keep in an airtight container for several weeks.

CHILLI CON VODKA

Whoever first had the idea of adding chocolate to chilli was a genius. And whoever had the idea of adding vodka was very bright as well. (Oh, right. That was me.)

Serves 6–8

225g (8oz) dried red kidney beans

2 tablespoons extra-virgin olive oil

1 tablespoon crushed garlic

4 tablespoons finely chopped onions

450g (1lb) lean minced beef

150ml (¼ pint) vodka

3 tablespoons *KGB Sauce* (see page 124)
   or hot red pepper sauce

4 small jalapeño chillies, chopped

1 teaspoon oregano

¾ teaspoon salt

50g (2oz) milk chocolate, minimum
   35 per cent cocoa solids

450ml (16fl oz) *Vodka Tomato Sauce*
   (see page 100)

1 teaspoon ground cumin

2 teaspoons paprika

Moscow Fry Bread (see page 128) or
   corn bread to serve

1 Soak the beans in cold water for 8–10 hours. Drain and rinse.

2 Heat the oil in a large saucepan and cook the garlic and onion until the onions become translucent.

3 Add the minced beef and cook until brown. Add the vodka and stir.

4 Add the beans and stir in the remaining ingredients in the order listed. Simmer for about 2 hours, uncovered.

5 Serve with *Moscow Fry Bread* or corn bread.

You can use tinned kidney beans to save time. Just rinse the beans quickly before using.

VODKA BEEF STROGANOFF WITH CHILLI SWEET POTATO CRISPS

I find it hard to believe that Count Pavel Alexandrovich Stroganov, a Russian diplomat, didn't drink vodka while dining on the dish that bears his name. So I find it fitting that this version puts the vodka right into the recipe.

Serves 6–8

1.1kg (2½lb) beef topside

1 tablespoon chilli powder

Salt and freshly ground black pepper, to taste

75g (3oz) butter

4 tablespoons plain flour

450g (1lb) onions, thinly sliced

225g (8oz) mushrooms, washed and sliced

1 teaspoon crushed garlic

350ml (12fl oz) *Vodka Beef Broth* (see page 127)

2 teaspoons Dijon mustard

125ml (4fl oz) sour cream

4 tablespoons vodka

1 tablespoon chopped fresh dill

1 Rinse the beef, pat dry and cut into 4 x 1cm (1½ x ½ in) strips. Season with the chilli powder, salt and pepper.

2 Heat 3 tablespoons of the butter in a large heavy-bottomed frying pan over a moderate-high heat.

3 Put 3 tablespoons of the flour in a bowl. Add the beef and toss to coat.

4 Transfer the beef to the pan and very quickly brown (just sear on all sides to seal in the juices; don't cook through). Transfer to a plate and set aside.

5 Reduce the heat to moderate and add another 3 tablespoons of the butter, the onions, mushrooms and garlic. Cook until the onions are soft.

6 Meanwhile, make a *roux* in a small saucepan by melting the rest of the butter over a moderate heat and whisking in the remaining flour. Cook until it becomes lightly browned and has a nutty aroma – about 3 minutes.

7 Add the *Vodka Beef Broth* and the mustard to the onion mixture and bring to a light boil, stirring constantly. Reduce to a simmer and stir in the *roux*.

8 Return the beef to the pan and add salt and black pepper to taste. Cover and simmer until the beef is cooked through and the liquid slightly reduced – about 10–15 minutes.

9 Stir in the sour cream, vodka and dill. Serve immediately, topped with *Chilli Sweet Potato Crisps*.

CHILLI SWEET POTATO CRISPS

2 sweet potatoes, peeled and very thinly sliced

450ml (16fl oz) vegetable oil

Salt, to taste

1 teaspoon chilli powder

1 Soak the raw potatoes slices in very cold water for about 30 minutes.

2 In a large deep-sided saucepan, heat the oil over a high heat. Drain the potatoes well and fry in batches. When the potatoes become crisp, remove them from the pan with a slotted spoon and lay in a dish lined with kitchen paper. Salt to taste, dust with the chilli powder and serve.

BLOODY NATASHA STEAKS

The roasted tomatoes and jalapeños in my Bloody Natasha recipe make this dish stand out.

Serves 4

4 sirloin steaks, about 225g (8oz) each

700ml (1¼ pints) *Bloody Natasha* (see page 151)

2 tablespoons canola or grapeseed oil

Coarse sea salt and freshly ground black pepper

2 tomatoes, halved

Baked potatoes, to serve

1 Place the steaks in a large re-sealable plastic bag with the *Bloody Natasha* and leave for 1–2 hours in the fridge, turning the bag a couple of times to ensure that the steaks are evenly coated.

2 Preheat a griddle pan over a high heat for about 10 minutes. Remove the steaks from the bag (reserving the marinade), pat dry, brush with the oil and season with salt and pepper. Cook to the desired doneness – about 5–6 minutes per side for medium, depending on thickness. (Remember to rotate the steaks 90° after about 2 minutes to create a cross-hatch of grill marks.) Allow the steaks to rest, covered, for about 4–5 minutes.

3 Griddle the tomatoes, cut-side down, for about 3–4 minutes.

4 Meanwhile, bring the reserved marinade to the boil in a small saucepan.

5 Transfer the steaks to warm plates and spoon the sauce on top. Garnish each plate with a grilled tomato half and serve with baked potatoes.

MONSTER MASH

Grain is mashed and fermented into raw spirit which is then triple distilled to remove impurities and produce high-proof, neutral grain spirit in Smirnoff 21.

Russians consider seafood to be a natural accompaniment to vodka – particularly salty fish like smoked herring. And caviar, all on its lonesome, just doesn't seem to tickle the palate the way it does when closely pursued by icy-chilled vodka.

Vodka can even be used to cure fish or to enhance a variety of cooking methods – from steaming to stir-frying. So with the assistance of a friendly fishmonger and these recipes at the ready, you and your guests will soon be hooked on several scintillating seafood dishes.

SEAFOOD

STONED CRAB CAKES WITH ORANGE VODKA PINEAPPLE SALSA

In my experience, many crab cakes are more cake than crab. But this version is light and flaky, using the minimum of breadcrumbs. Sometimes I also start out by steaming the crabs with a little vodka – in a similar manner to that which I use in the Lobsters Steamed in Vodka later in this chapter. But the kick in this dish comes from the spicy salsa.

Makes about 10–12

150g (5oz) raw or cooked prawns

1½ teaspoons coarse salt

Orange Vodka Pineapple Salsa (see recipe right)

225g (8oz) loaf white bread, crusts removed, chopped into small cubes

3 tablespoons *Lemon Peel Vodka* (see page 142)

1 tablespoon butter

1 large egg white

Freshly ground black pepper, to taste

2 tablespoons double cream

1 tablespoon finely chopped red chilli

1 tablespoon finely chopped coriander

1 tablespoon finely chopped spring onions, white part only

1 teaspoon very finely chopped fresh ginger

225g (8oz) crabmeat

250ml (9fl oz) vegetable or corn oil

1 Preheat the oven to 150°C/300°F/gas mark 2.

2 Peel and de-vein the prawns and submerge in iced water with 1 teaspoon of coarse salt for about 30–60 minutes.

3 Prepare the *Orange Vodka Pineapple Salsa* and chill.

4 Place the bread cubes on a baking tray and bake until the bread is crisp, but not brown – about 6–8 minutes. Put the toasted cubes in a blender and pulse into coarse breadcrumbs. Transfer to a large bowl and set aside.

5 Drain the prawns and pat dry with kitchen paper. Place in a blender or food-processor with the vodka and butter and whizz to a smooth purée; set aside.

6 Lightly whisk the egg white with the remaining salt and black pepper in a large bowl. Add the prawns, cream, chopped chilli, coriander, spring onions and ginger and mix until thoroughly combined.

7 Finally, fold the crabmeat into the prawn mixture.

8 Using your hands, scoop up about 2 heaped tablespoons of crab mixture and gently roll it in the breadcrumbs until it is completely covered and forms a small ball. Pick it up and press the ball between your palms into a small cake – about 8cm (3in) in diameter – then carefully rest it on a platter or baking tray. Repeat with the remainder of the crab mixture.

9 Pour the oil into a deep-sided pan or fryer on a high heat. Fry the crab cakes in batches (do not crowd), turning just once, until they are golden – about for 3–4 minutes on each side. Remove the crab cakes with a slotted spoon and drain on kitchen paper. Serve with the *Orange Vodka Pineapple Salsa*.

ORANGE VODKA PINEAPPLE SALSA

Makes about 250ml (9fl oz)

225g (8oz) fresh pineapple, finely chopped
1 tablespoon finely chopped red chilli,
    de-seeded
4 tablespoons *Orange Peel Vodka* (see
    page 142)
1 tablespoon *Apple Vodka* (see page 143)
2 tablespoons freshly squeezed lime juice
½ teaspoon *KGB Sauce* (see page 124),
    or hot red pepper sauce (optional)
1 teaspoon finely chopped fresh ginger
Salt and freshly ground black pepper,
    to taste

1 Combine all the ingredients in a small bowl and chill until ready to serve.

SALMON BEGGAR'S PURSE WITH VODKA AND PEPPER CREAM

This is a rather elegant and light little dish that always seems to impress – both the eyes and the palate.

Makes 6

450ml (16fl oz) *Vodka Cream Sauce*
    (see page 104)
1 tablespoon black peppercorns
450g (1lb) skinless salmon steak
4 tablespoons extra-virgin olive oil
Coarse sea salt and freshly ground black
    or white pepper, to taste
4 tablespoons *Lemon Peel Vodka* (see
    page 142)
6 crêpes (see page 23)
2 hard-boiled eggs
110g (4oz) red onions, thinly sliced
110g (4oz) capers
Blanched long chives, to tie the purses

1 Prepare the *Vodka Cream Sauce*, purée and add the peppercorns. Keep warm.

2 Rinse the salmon, pat dry, rub with 2 tablespoons of the olive oil and season with salt and pepper.

3 Heat a large heavy-bottomed frying pan over a moderate heat and add the salmon. Cook until the centre becomes translucent – about 3–4 minutes each side. Deglaze the pan by adding the vodka. Remove from the heat and, when cool enough to handle, cut the steaks into 5cm (2in) pieces; return to the pan (to continue to soak up the vodka) and set aside.

4 Prepare the crêpes.

5 Boil the eggs. Peel the eggs and separately chop the yolks and whites. Set aside.

6 To assemble, lay a crêpe on your work surface, place a piece of the salmon on the crêpe, sprinkle with the red onions, capers and eggs and season with salt and pepper.

7 Gather the crêpe at the top and tie with a long chive; it should resemble a bag or purse.

8 To serve, spoon a circle of the warm *Vodka Cream Sauce* on each plate and set a Beggar's Purse on top.

LOBSTERS STEAMED IN VODKA WITH VODKA TARRAGON DIPPING SAUCE

Next time you steam lobsters at home, try this variation. The Vodka Tarragon Dipping Sauce is well worth the extra effort.

Serves 2–4

175ml (6fl oz) vodka

175ml (6fl oz) water

2–4 live lobsters

2 large lemons, 1 cut into wedges

50g (20oz) unsalted butter, in pieces

½ teaspoon dried tarragon

Salt, to taste

1 Bring the vodka and water to a rapid boil in a large lidded saucepan. Add the lobsters, cover and return to the boil. Cook for 16–18 minutes.

2 Remove the lobsters with tongs and reserve the liquid.

3 Holding the lobsters with tongs over the pan, clip the tips off the claws with kitchen shears and let the water drain out. Separate the tails and claws from the bodies and rinse under warm water. Run a sharp knife down the length of each lobster tail and arrange each lobster on a plate with a lemon wedge.

4 Pour the reserved liquid into a medium saucepan and boil down until about 175ml (6fl oz) remains. Pass the mixture through a sieve, return to the pan and whisk in the cold butter, piece by piece.

5 Add the tarragon, juice from 1 lemon and salt to taste. Serve the sauce in small bowls with the lobsters, baked potatoes and/or steamed corn on the cob.

SPICY STIR-FRIED PRAWNS WITH VODKA AND MANGO

This recipe could not be simpler and comes together very quickly. It is meant to be a very spicy dish. But you can reduce the heat by cutting back on the hot red pepper sauce. You can also substitute pineapple for mango.

Serves 4

700g (1½lb) prawns, peeled and de-veined

3 tablespoons freshly squeezed lemon juice

1 teaspoon *KGB Sauce* (see page 124) or hot red pepper sauce.

1 tablespoon vegetable oil

1 tablespoon butter

1 hot chilli, finely chopped

25g (1oz) shallots, finely chopped

½ teaspoon very finely chopped ginger

1 teaspoon crushed garlic

4 tablespoons *Lemon Peel Vodka* (see page 142)

225g (8oz) mango, peeled and chopped

2 tablespoons finely chopped coriander

1 Place the prawns in a bowl with the lemon juice, *KGB Sauce* and salt and pepper to taste. Cover and refrigerate for 30 minutes.

2 Heat the oil and the butter together in a large wok over a high heat and add the chilli, shallots, ginger and garlic. Toss and cook for 1–2 minutes.

3 Add the prawns and toss rapidly for about 2–3 minutes.

4 Add the vodka and mango and toss just long enough to warm the mango.

5 Add the coriander, toss once and immediately transfer to a platter and serve with steamed white rice.

SALMON STRANNIK

'Strannik' (pronounced 'stra-neek') is the Russian word for hobo or wandering soul. This dish is best served outdoors, cooked on a campfire or grill – strannik-style. Cooked entirely in foil in its own juices, this self-contained meal packs light in a small cooler and leaves no clean-up. Of course, it can also be cooked in your oven at home. But it's not nearly as much fun as turning out a posh dish while seated with friends around an open fire.

Serves 4

4 salmon fillets, rinsed and patted dry

Coarse salt and freshly ground black
    pepper, to taste

125ml (4fl oz) *Lemon Peel Vodka* (see
    page 142)

50ml (2fl oz) extra-virgin olive oil

1 large carrot, sliced into thin ribbons

4 shallots, thinly sliced

1 garlic clove, bruised

2 tablespoons freshly squeezed lemon
    juice

50g (2oz) butter, quartered

6–8 fresh thyme sprigs

4 tablespoons dry white wine

2 tablespoons double cream

1 large lemon, cut into wedges, to serve

1 Season the salmon well with salt and pepper, place in a re-sealable plastic bag with the *Lemon Peel Vodka* and olive oil and marinate in the fridge for about 1 hour.

2 Lay out 2 sheets of heavy-duty aluminium foil, each about 60cm (2ft) in length, one on top of the other.

3 Place the carrot in a single layer in the centre of the foil, then add the shallots and garlic.

4 Remove the salmon from the plastic bag (discard the marinade) and place the fish over the shallots. Season the fish with more salt and pepper and top with the lemon juice, butter and thyme. Pour the white wine over the whole lot and drizzle with the cream.

5 Lay a third length of heavy-duty foil over the top. Tightly roll the edges of the sheets together on all sides, snuggly enclosing the contents. Lastly, enclose the whole pack in a final layer of foil and refrigerate until ready to cook.

6 Clear a place among the white coals of a barbecue or grill. Place the packet in the cleared area and enclose – but don't cover – with glowing coals. Cook for about 30 minutes – making sure you keep the packet surrounded by hot coals. (Alternatively, you can cook the packet in the oven preheated to 150°C/300°F/gas mark 2 for about the same time.)

7 Remove from the coals and open (take care to avoid the hot burst of steam as you break the seal). Serve with lemon wedges to squeeze over each portion.

HABAÑERO-ENCRUSTED TUNA WITH LEMON VODKA AND THYME DRESSING

If you like it spicy, this is the dish for you. The habañero is one of the hottest chillies in the world. But, used sparingly, it conveys a wonderful flavour without setting your face on fire.

Serves 4

Lemon Vodka and Thyme Dressing (see
    recipe below)

4 tuna steaks, about 225g (8oz) each

225ml (8fl oz) *Lemon Peel Vodka* (see
    page 142)

75g (3oz) flour

2 tablespoons dried habeñero chilli flakes
    or powder

1 teaspoon salt

1 tablespoon freshly ground black pepper

1 teaspoon ground fennel

1 teaspoon dried thyme

1 teaspoon dried basil

1 teaspoon dried marjoram

1 teaspoon dried rosemary

2 eggs, lightly beaten

3 tablespoons canola or grapeseed oil

3 tablespoons unsalted butter

4 fresh thyme sprigs to garnish

Stir-fried vegetables and steamed rice,
    to serve

1 Prepare the *Lemon Vodka and Thyme Dressing*.

2 Rinse the tuna steaks, lightly score the flesh with a sharp knife and marinate in the vodka for about 1 hour in the fridge, turning occasionally.

3 Combine the flour in a medium bowl with the habañero, salt, pepper and all the dried herbs.

4 Pat the tuna dry, discarding the vodka, and dip each steak in the eggs; then dredge in the flour mixture until completely coated.

5 Heat the oil in a large heavy-bottomed frying pan over a high heat. Add the butter and cook the tuna steaks (turning once) until opaque and evenly browned – about 6–8 minutes.

6 Transfer the steaks to 4 warm plates, drizzle with the *Lemon Vodka and Thyme Dressing* and garnish with the thyme sprigs. Serve with stir-fried vegetables and/or rice.

LEMON VODKA AND THYME DRESSING

Makes about 175ml (6fl oz)

4 fresh thyme sprigs

125ml (4fl oz) extra-virgin olive oil

125ml (4fl oz) *Lemon Peel Vodka* (see
    page 142)

1 tablespoon *KGB Sauce* (see page 124),
    or hot red pepper sauce

Salt and freshly ground black pepper,
    to taste

1 Bruise the thyme with the flat side of a chef's knife and combine all the ingredients in a small saucepan. Cook over a low heat for about 10 minutes. Cover and leave to stand for about 1 hour.

2 Strain the mixture through a sieve lined with cheesecloth and discard the solids.

3 Serve immediately or store in an airtight jar until ready to use.

PASTA

Sunday was always pasta day in my house. Come to think of it, so were Monday and Wednesday (and every Friday during Lent). Sunday mornings I would awake to the smell of tomato sauce (or 'gravy' as my East Boston-bred family insisted on calling it) and meats frying. We always had a late afternoon pasta dinner – with plenty of sauce to re-use later in the week.

If I spent the night at my grandmother's (my Sicilian 'Nonny'), I might also find most available flat surfaces (even the beds) covered with row upon row of fresh stuffed pasta. From the time I could walk, I was called into service to help seal the cheese ravioli edges with a fork. And every family feast featured those exquisite Italian dumplings. So I have very strong and fond associations of my family with pasta.

The addition of vodka to pasta sauce was an evolutionary process. I first tried adding vodka to some time-worn recipes. Then I started researching and crafting sauces that were best complemented by vodka. The result is several reliable basic sauces and a handful of recipes that I now count among my favourites.

KREMLIN PASTA

You could add this sauce to just about any pasta – rigatoni or penne, for example. But I find the Red Star Pasta to be a fun alternative to conventional shapes and colours, giving this dish a unique visual character in addition to its hearty flavour.

Serves 4–6

Red Star Pasta (see recipe below)

450ml (16fl oz) *Vodka Tomato Sauce*
(see page 100)

225g (8 oz) *Over-heated Tomatoes*
(see page 33) or sun-dried tomatoes,
sliced

40g (1½oz) fresh basil leaves

225ml (8fl oz) ricotta cheese

110g (4oz) Parmesan-Reggiano, grated

4 tablespoons vodka

2 teaspoons freshly ground black pepper

1 teaspoon icing sugar

2 tablespoons salt

1 Prepare the *Red Star Pasta* and set aside.

2 Bring the *Vodka Tomato Sauce* to a simmer in a medium heavy-bottomed frying pan and add the *Over-heated Tomatoes*. Return to a simmer, add about half the basil leaves and cover the pan.

3 In a medium bowl, mix together the ricotta, Parmesan, vodka, black pepper and icing sugar until smooth.

4 Bring a large saucepan of salted water to the boil. Drop the pasta into the boiling water and cook until it starts to float on the surface – about 1 minute. Immediately drain the pasta in a colander and add to the tomato sauce. Toss or stir until well-coated and serve immediately topped with scoops of the cheese mixture, garnished with the remaining basil leaves.

RED STAR PASTA

Inspired by the Soviet red stars that still adorn the Kremlin in Moscow, the star shapes add a little whimsy to any pasta course. This can be prepared the day before and kept in the fridge. Or freeze it in an airtight container and it will last for weeks.

2 eggs

1 tablespoon extra-virgin olive oil

4 tablespoons tomato paste

1 tablespoon *KGB Sauce* (see page 124)

½ teaspoon salt

250g (9oz) flour, plus extra for working dough

Star-shaped cookie cutter, approximately 5cm (2in)

1 Beat the eggs in a small bowl and mix in the olive oil, tomato paste, *KGB Sauce* and salt. Set aside.

2 Tip the flour into a large bowl. Create a well in the middle of the flour and slowly add the egg mixture to the well. Stir the egg mixture using a fork, allowing it to slowly incorporate only enough of the flour to create a sticky dough. If the dough is too dry, add more tomato paste; if too wet, add more flour.

3 Turn the dough onto a work surface or board dusted with flour and knead it with the heel of your hand – allowing it to incorporate more flour until it becomes elastic, smooth and evenly coloured. Roll the dough into a ball, cover in cling film and leave to rest for 15 minutes.

4 Again dust your work surface with flour and roll out the dough to a thickness of 6mm (¼in). Cut the dough into stars using a cookie cutter. Gather up the excess dough, roll out again and repeat until you have made as many red stars as possible. As you finish the stars, lay them on a large baking tray or sheet – dusted with plenty of flour to keep them from sticking together and covered with a clean, dry tea towel.

VODKA RED PESTO SAUCE

Vodka Red Pesto can be added to any pasta, like penne or linguine. Or you can use it to top fresh mozzarella cheese, sandwiches or soups (like minestrone).

Makes about 225ml (8fl oz)

3 garlic cloves

3 tablespoons pine nuts

175g (6oz) fresh basil leaves, torn into
  fine shreds

2 tablespoons extra-virgin olive oil

8 Over-heated Tomatoes (see page 33)
  or sun-dried tomatoes, chopped

4 tablespoons vodka

Salt and freshly ground black pepper

450g (1lb) pasta of your choice

2 tablespoons Romano cheese, grated

3 tablespoons Parmesan-Reggiano, grated
  (and extra for topping)

Fresh basil, chopped, to garnish

1 Put the garlic, pine nuts, basil and oil in a blender or food-processor and pulse to a smooth paste.

2 Add the chopped tomatoes and pulse until they too have been completely incorporated.

3 Finally, drizzle in the vodka and add salt and pepper to taste.

4 Meanwhile, bring a large saucepan of lightly salted water to the boil. Add the pasta and cook until *al dente*. Strain, reserving about 4 tablespoons of water, and return to the pan.

5 Add the basil mixture to the pasta and stir in. If it is too dry, add some of the reserved pasta water and/or olive oil.

6 Toss with the grated cheeses and serve immediately – garnished with basil and more Parmesan, if desired.

Vodka Red Pesto Sauce is best stored at room temperature. The sauce will last 2–3 days at room temperature and 4–7 days in the fridge. It can also be stored in the freezer for a month or more: pour the pesto into a sterilised jar and add a 6mm (¼in) layer of olive oil to the top. Press a piece of clingfilm over the jar, allowing the wrap to hang over the sides. Screw on the lid and freeze immediately. Thaw to room temperature before adding to a recipe. If the pesto flavour has dulled, try adding a dash of good–quality balsamic vinegar to round it out.

Do not heat the pesto sauce separately – the basil may blacken and/or taste bitter. Also, it shouldn't be too hot. It is usually best to just let the heat from the freshly cooked pasta do the job of warming it.

VODKA TOMATO SAUCE

In addition to being great over just about any pasta, this sauce is a perfect base to more complex sauces and soups, to make Chilli con Vodka (see page 81), or use it as a simple pizza topping.

Makes about 1 litre (1¾ pints)

500g (1lb) fresh plum tomatoes
½ teaspoon salt
2 tablespoons extra-virgin olive oil
6 large garlic cloves, bruised
110g (4oz) onions, finely chopped
4 tablespoons *Basil Vodka* (see page 146) or vodka
2 tablespoons finely chopped flat-leaf parsley
½ teaspoon *KGB Sauce* (see page 124), or hot red pepper sauce
1 teaspoon sugar
Salt and freshly ground black pepper, to taste

1 Wash and score the tops of the tomatoes with a cross and cover with boiling, salted water. Remove the tomatoes and plunge them into very cold or iced water to stop them from cooking.
2 Peel the tomatoes (the skin should easily slide off), slice them in half lengthways, squeeze or push out all the seeds and finely chop the flesh. Set aside.

3 Heat the oil in a large saucepan over a moderate heat. Add the bruised garlic to the pan and cook until golden – about 3–4 minutes.
4 Add the onions and cook until soft – about 4–5 minutes. Remove the garlic.
5 Add the tomatoes and the remaining ingredients, bring to the boil and then simmer uncovered, stirring frequently, for about 30 minutes – producing a chunky sauce.

Always use a non-reactive pan (never aluminium or copper) when cooking tomato sauces (or any acidic foods) to avoid metals leaching into the sauce.

You can substitute tinned, peeled whole plum tomatoes for the fresh tomatoes. Just drain the excess juice, de-seed and finely chop, then proceed to step 3.

To create a smoother consistency more suitable for some recipes, pass the cooked sauce through a mouli or pulse a few times in a blender or food-processor. But do not purée.

This sauce can be stored in an airtight container in the fridge for up to a week, or frozen for several months.

LINGUINE WITH VODKA RED CLAM SAUCE

This is adapted from an old family recipe. The original Sicilian ingredients did not include vodka. But after cooking this recipe dozens of times over the years, I have concluded that the addition of vodka is a subtle yet definite improvement on the distinct flavour of the dish.

Serves 4

4 plum tomatoes
Salt and freshly ground black pepper
2 tablespoons crushed garlic
2 tablespoons extra-virgin olive oil
50g (2oz) tinned anchovy fillets
4 tablespoons *Basil Vodka* (see page 146) or vodka
225g (8oz) clams, chopped and juice reserved
1 teaspoon *KGB Sauce* (see page 124) or red pepper flakes
1 teaspoon sugar
1 tablespoon dried basil
450g (1lb) linguine
Fresh basil leaves, to garnish

1 Wash and score the tops of the tomatoes with a cross and cook for 1 minute in enough boiling water to cover plus ½ teaspoon salt. Remove the tomatoes and plunge into very cold or iced water to stop them from cooking. Peel, seed and chop the tomatoes and set aside.

2 Cook the garlic in the oil in a large saucepan over a moderate heat for about 2 minutes (do not brown).

3 Add the anchovies to the pan and, using a wooden spoon, mash the anchovies and garlic into a paste.

4 Add the *Basil Vodka* to the paste and stir (watch out for splatter). Immediately add the clams with their juice, plus about 225ml (8fl oz) water. Bring to the boil and cook until reduced by about a quarter – about 15 minutes.

5 Add the tomatoes, *KGB Sauce*, sugar, pepper and dried basil.

6 Simmer, uncovered, for 30 minutes, stirring frequently.

7 Meanwhile, bring a large saucepan of water to the boil. Do not salt. Add the pasta and cook until *al dente*. Do not drain.

8 Instead, using tongs or a pasta server, transfer the pasta directly to bowls.

9 Ladle a generous amount of sauce over the pasta and serve garnished with basil leaves.

VERMICELLI WITH VODKA LEMON CREAM SAUCE

This dish takes only minutes to make – no longer than it takes to boil the pasta. Though it's great on its own, in half portions it also makes a fine starter or side dish.

Serves 4–6

1 tablespoon salt
450g (1lb) vermicelli
1 garlic clove
110g (4oz) unsalted butter
1 lemon, sliced
4 tablespoons *Lemon Peel Vodka* (see page 142)
125ml (4fl oz) cream
Fresh parsley, to garnish
225g (8oz) Parmesan-Reggiano, grated, to serve

1 Bring a large saucepan of water to the boil. Add the salt and vermicelli and cook until nearly *al dente*. Drain.

2 Meanwhile, sauté the garlic in the butter in a large saucepan over a moderate heat; when the garlic browns, discard it – about 5–7 minutes.

3 Add the lemon slices to the butter and cook for about 5 minutes. Reduce the heat to low and stir in the *Lemon Peel Vodka* and cream. Immediately add the drained vermicelli, toss and garnish with parsley. Serve immediately with the Parmesan.

Dos and don'ts of boiling pasta

Do use lots and lots of water; it keeps pasta from sticking together. Don't add oil to the water; it prevents the sauce from adhering to the pasta.

Do add plenty of salt to the water (unless the recipe directs you otherwise) as pasta has little flavour of its own.

Don't overcook pasta. Pasta should always be served *al dente* – tender but still firm (just like me). To test, remove a piece of pasta with tongs or a slotted spoon. Let it cool slightly, then taste. Remember that fresh pasta cooks much faster than dried pasta – often in just 2–3 minutes.

TAGLIATELLE WITH SAUSAGE AND VODKA TOMATO SAUCE

Fresh or dry ribbons of tagliatelle perfectly complement this hearty dish. If you can buy fresh Italian sausage links from a butcher, use them. Otherwise, the recipe for Sausage Patties (right) is hard to beat and one you will undoubtedly find other uses for – including my Eggs Benedict with Vodka Citrus Chilli Hollandaise Sauce (see page 24).

Serves 4

1 tablespoon extra-virgin olive oil

4 garlic cloves, minced

6 *Sausage Patties* (see recipe right) or
    6 Italian sausages, chopped

1 litre (1¾ pints) *Vodka Tomato Sauce*
    (see page 100)

1 teaspoon *KGB Sauce* (see page 124)
    or ½ teaspoon red chilli flakes

4 tablespoons vodka

125ml (4fl oz) double cream

450g (1lb) tagliatelle

Salt

Fresh parsley, to garnish

1 Heat the oil over a moderate heat in a large heavy-bottomed frying pan. Add the garlic and chopped sausage to the pan and cook until brown – about 3–5 minutes for cooked sausage patties; about 10 minutes for chopped fresh sausage.

2 Add the *Vodka Tomato Sauce* and the *KGB Sauce* to the pan and bring to the boil. Stir in the vodka and cream, reduce the heat and simmer for 15 minutes.

3 Meanwhile, bring a large saucepan of lightly salted water to the boil. Add the pasta and cook until nearly *al dente* (it will continue to cook in the sauce).

4 Using tongs or a pasta server, transfer the pasta, a little at a time, to the sauce. Toss or stir to coat thoroughly. Serve garnished with fresh parsley.

SAUSAGE PATTIES

Makes 8

450g (1lb) freshly minced pork

2 tablespoons freshly chopped parsley

1 tablespoon freshly chopped basil

½ teaspoon dried oregano

2 teaspoons crushed garlic

2 teaspoons paprika

1 teaspoon crushed fennel seeds

1 teaspoon *KGB Sauce* (see page 124) or
   ½ teaspoon crushed red chilli flakes

1 teaspoon freshly ground black pepper

1 teaspoon salt

2 pinches of grated nutmeg

2 tablespoons extra-virgin olive oil

1 Mix thoroughly all the ingredients except the oil, then divide into 8 equal portions and form into round patties.

2 Heat the oil in large heavy-bottomed frying pan. Add the patties (in batches if necessary) and brown on both sides, turning regularly, until they are cooked through and no longer pink inside.

3 Transfer the patties to a plate lined with kitchen paper to absorb excess oil.

PENNE AND VODKA CREAM SAUCE

There are numerous variations of this classic – probably the only vodka entrée I've seen served in restaurants. Since I'm not a big fan of rich cream sauces I experimented until I arrived at this light and flavourful version.

**Serves 4 as a main course
(or 8 as a starter)**

350g (12oz) plum tomatoes

Salt and freshly ground white pepper,
   to taste

40g (1½oz) butter

110g (4oz) pancetta, chopped

225g (8oz) onions, finely chopped

2 large garlic cloves, bruised

4 tablespoons vodka

1 teaspoon *KGB Sauce* (see page 124)
   or 1 teaspoon red chilli flakes

125ml (4fl oz) double cream

450g (1lb) penne

2 tablespoons extra-virgin olive oil

2–3 tablespoons freshly chopped parsley
   or basil

175g (6oz) fresh Parmesan-Reggiano,
   shaved

1 Wash and score the tops of the tomatoes with a cross and cover with boiling, salted water. Remove the tomatoes and plunge them into very cold or iced water to stop them from cooking. Peel, seed and chop the tomatoes and set aside.

2 Melt the butter in a large, heavy-bottomed frying pan over a moderate heat. Add the pancetta and sauté until lightly browned – about 5–7 minutes.

3 Add the onions and garlic and cook until the onions are softened – about 5 minutes.

4 Remove the garlic, add the tomatoes, vodka and *KGB Sauce* or chilli flakes and simmer, uncovered, for about 10–12 minutes – stirring every few minutes. Stir in the cream and add salt and pepper to taste.

5 Meanwhile, bring a large saucepan of lightly salted water to the boil. Add the pasta and cook until nearly *al dente* (it will continue to cook in the sauce).

6 Drain the pasta and add it to the sauce. Mix thoroughly and continue to heat until the pasta is *al dente*.

7 Swirl in the olive oil and serve garnished with chopped parsley or basil, with the parmesan on the side.

You can find pancetta in many supermarkets or any Italian deli. Pancetta is spicy-sweet Italian cured pork – similar to bacon – often used in stews, sauces and stuffings. If you must substitute smoked bacon for pancetta, first blanch it by boiling in water for just a few seconds to subdue the smoky flavour.

NAKED RAVIOLI IN VODKA TOMATO SAUCE

Ravioli were always a feature of family feasts at Christmas and other holidays. I would always hunt near the bottom of the bowl for a few of the loose fillings – the 'naked ravioli' – that would break from the pasta. In this recipe, the actual pasta is omitted altogether to create light ricotta dumplings that literally melt in your mouth.

Serves 6–8

1 tablespoon salt

175g (6oz) Parmesan-Reggiano, grated

900g (2lb) ricotta cheese, drained

110g (4oz) flour

3 tablespoons *Basil Vodka* (see page 146) or vodka

3 tablespoons freshly chopped flat-leaf parsley

¼ teaspoon freshly grated nutmeg

1 tablespoon sugar

10g (½oz) butter, melted

Salt and freshly ground black pepper

25g (1oz) fresh basil, torn into small pieces to garnish

1 litre (1¾ pints) *Vodka Tomato Sauce* (see page 100), warmed

1 Bring about 4 litres (8 pints) of water to the boil in a large saucepan with the salt.

2 In a large bowl, blend 4 tablespoons of the parmesan with the ricotta, flour, *Basil Vodka* or vodka, parsley, nutmeg, sugar, butter, 1 teaspoon salt and ½ teaspoon pepper. Add only enough flour to the mixture to transform it into a very loose dough.

3 Take a large spoonful of the ricotta mixture, roll it into a ball and drop it into the boiling water.

4 When the ball floats to the surface – after about 45 seconds – remove it with a slotted spoon. If the ball holds together, form the remainder of the mixture into balls and drop into the boiling water in batches of 8 or 10. If the ball falls apart, add more flour to the mix and test until the ball holds together before you proceed with the rest of the mixture.

5 Lay the cooked naked ravioli in one layer on a platter.

6 Stir the fresh basil into the warm *Vodka Tomato Sauce* and pour over the ravioli. Top with the remaining Parmesan and serve.

If the ricotta is too soft or runny, it must be drained before you begin or the ravioli will absorb too much flour. Simply suspend the ricotta in a sieve or cheesecloth over a bowl for up to 24 hours in the fridge.

Charcoal has amazing absorption qualities and has been used for centuries to purify vodka. Only silver birch or oak hardwood, specially selected from sustainable forests in Poland, is used in the production of Smirnoff No. 21 vodka.

FOREST
FILTER

DESSERTS

Vodka and sweet things seem to have a natural affinity for each other. Vodka is commonly paired with fruit juices and other sugary mixers, for example, so I guess it should come as no surprise that this chapter grew faster and larger than the others.

In addition to the obvious zing vodka brings to so many dishes, it also adds an exquisite balance and complexity to desserts. In many cases, its presence can be nearly imperceptible, and it often goes unnoticed. But vodka serves to mellow sweetness and add a light airy texture to these decadent dishes. And where infused vodka is used, an additional burst of flavour is injected.

So, if you've been very good and eaten all your vodka dinner, you may turn the page

VODKA BERRIES ROMANOFF

Here is another Russian-inspired classic – with a vodka spin, of course. The original dish is attributed to French pastry chef Marie-Antoine Careme (1784–1833) who cooked for the Romanoff family in Russia – including Russian Tsar Nicholas I.

Serves 4–6

550g (1lb) strawberries or mixed berries
1 tablespoon icing sugar
1 tablespoon lemon juice
4 tablespoons *Orange Peel Vodka* (see page 142) or vodka
125ml (4fl oz) sour cream
225ml (8fl oz) vanilla ice cream, softened
225ml (8fl oz) *Lemon Vodka Whipped Cream* (see page 119)
2 tablespoons shredded fresh mint leaves

1 Wash, hull and dry the strawberries or rinse the berries. Toss in the sugar and lemon juice and arrange on a serving platter.
2 Whisk together the *Orange Peel Vodka* and sour cream in a large mixing bowl. Stir in the ice cream and fold in the *Lemon Vodka Whipped Cream*.
3 Pour the cream mixture on top of the berries or serve on the side. Decorate with fresh mint.

CHERRY VODKA CRÈME BRÛLÉE

In addition to the vodka, this version of crème brûlée is unique because of the syrupy layer of vodka-steeped cherries that sits below the rich, creamy custard.

Serves 6

400g (14oz) fresh or frozen and defrosted sour cherries, stoned (sour cherries, which are sometimes called tart red cherries or pie cherries, are harvested in summer and usually frozen, tinned or dried; if you want to use fresh ones, your best bet is a farmer's market)

110g (4oz) granulated sugar, plus extra for the caramel glaze

125ml (4fl oz) *Sour Cherry Vodka* (see page 146) or vodka

600ml (1 pint) double cream

¼ teaspoon salt

9 egg yolks

1 Preheat the oven to 140°C/275°F/gas mark 1.

2 Cook the cherries with the sugar in a medium saucepan over a moderate heat until the cherries are soft and the liquid is syrupy – about 10 minutes. Add the *Sour Cherry Vodka* and remove from the heat. Distribute about half of this mixture in the bottom of 6 custard cups or ramekins.

3 Add the cream and salt to the remainder of the cherry/vodka mixture, bring to a simmer and remove from the heat.

4 Lightly beat the egg yolks in a large mixing bowl.

5 Add a few tablespoons of the cherry/vodka/cream mixture to the eggs (this will temper them to the heat) and mix thoroughly. Then slowly whisk the remainder of the mixture into the eggs.

6 Pass through a fine sieve and very gently pour into the custard cups.

7 Space the cups apart in a roasting tin (they should not touch each other or the sides of the tin), then add enough boiling water to the tin to reach about half-way up the sides of the cups. Bake until the custard becomes set, but still 'jiggly' in the centre – about 1 hour. Leave to cool to room temperature and then chill for at least 8 hours (up to 24) in your fridge.

8 Sprinkle a fine layer of granulated sugar over the top of each custard and caramelise using a chef's blowtorch or directly under a hot grill. If you wish, serve with more *Sour Cherry Vodka* on the side and/or drizzled over the top.

When available, I sometimes mix fresh cherries with cherry vodka and sugar and marinate in my fridge overnight. I then spoon the cherries on top of each crème brûlée just as I serve them.

RED SQUARES

House parties and vodka jellies – vodka and flavoured gelatine set in small squeezable paper cups – are a fond memory of my years in Boston. I've dressed them up and given them a Moscow spin. But this jiggly wiggly concoction is just as much fun now that I spend more time near Red Square than Copley Square.

Serves 4

110g (4oz) strawberry jelly

225ml (8fl oz) *Lemon Peel Vodka* (see
page 142)

Fresh mint to decorate

Icing sugar, for dusting (optional)

1 Mix the jelly in a medium bowl with 450ml (16fl oz) boiling water, or as per the instructions on the packet, until the jelly has completely dissolved.

2 Stir in half the *Lemon Peel Vodka* and pour into a 12 x 20cm (5 x 8in) tin. Refrigerate until firm – about 4 hours.

3 Dip the bottom of the tin and a small knife into warm water for about 15 seconds. Use the knife to cut the gelatine into 2½cm (1in) squares. Serve in chilled martini glasses garnished with mint. Dust with icing sugar, if desired.

PLUMS ON FIRE

This is the 'ooohs' and 'ahhhs' dessert in my house. Because those are the sounds my son makes when he (from a safe distance) watches me pour flaming lemon vodka over sugared plums.

Serves 6–8

110g (4oz) almonds, halved

225g (8oz) sugar

1 tablespoon finely chopped fresh ginger

2 tablespoons freshly squeezed orange juice

900g (2lb) plums, halved and stoned

4 tablespoons *Lemon Peel Vodka* (see page 142)

2 teaspoons *Vanilla Vodka* (see page 143) or vanilla extract

Vanilla Vodka Whipped Cream (see page 119), to serve

1 Toast the almonds in a small sauté pan over a moderate-high heat until they turn golden brown – about 5 minutes. Set aside.

2 Combine the sugar, ginger and orange juice with 125ml (4fl oz) water in a large saucepan. Bring to the boil, then immediately lower the heat and simmer, stirring frequently, until the sugar has completely dissolved – about 10 minutes.

3 Add the plums to the syrup and cook until they are tender but firm – about 10–15 minutes. Remove with a slotted spoon and transfer to a heat-resistant serving dish.

4 Bring the syrup to the boil, pour over the plums and leave to cool.

5 When ready to serve, put both vodkas in a saucepan, quickly bring to a simmer and ignite.

6 Pour over the plums, sprinkle with the toasted almonds and serve with the *Vanilla Vodka Whipped Cream*.

LEMON/LIME VODKA GRANITA

Growing up in Boston, summertime was always punctuated by trips to the local 'slush' stall, as we called it, for a cup of soft lemon ice. Later I realised why so many adults loved the stuff as much as us kids – they were adding vodka to their slush. Here it is all dressed up.

Serves 4

Grated zest of 1 lime

225ml (8fl oz) freshly squeezed lemon juice

4 tablespoons freshly squeezed lime juice

125ml (4fl oz) *Vodka Simple Syrup* (see page 129)

4 tablespoons *Lemon Peel Vodka* or vodka (see page 142)

Fresh berries, to decorate

1 Combine the lime zest, juices, syrup and *Lemon Peel Vodka* and transfer to a metal 32.5 x 23cm (13 x 9in) baking tin. Freeze for 4 hours.

2 Remove the tin from the freezer and scrape the surface with a sturdy fork to create large... umm... scrapings.

3 Transfer the scrapings to chilled martini glasses or wine goblets and decorate with fresh berries or try *Twisted Citrus* (see page 119) slices rolled in sugar.

CHOCOLATE LOAF WITH ESPRESSO VODKA GLAZE

Everybody doesn't like something. But nobody doesn't like this chocolate loaf. The vodka helps the cake go a bit gooey inside and perhaps sag a little in the middle. (Vodka sometimes has the same effect on me, as a matter of fact.) But there's no denying how tasty it is. And the Espresso Vodka Glaze adds a sweet coffee finish. There are lots of chocolate recipes out there. Mine is inspired by Nigella Lawson's Dense Chocolate Cake from her book 'How to Be a Domestic Goddess'. Cheers, Nigella.

Serves 8–10 (or 1, if you don't like to share)

175g (6oz) flour

1 teaspoon baking powder

110g (4oz) dark chocolate, minimum 35 per cent cocoa solids

5 tablespoons vodka

225g (8oz) butter, softened

300g (10½oz) dark brown sugar

2 large eggs, beaten

2 teaspoons *Vanilla Vodka* (see page 143) or vanilla extract

175ml (6fl oz) boiling water

100g (3½oz) icing sugar

⅛ teaspoon salt

2 tablespoons *Espresso Vodka* (see page 145) or 2 tablespoons vodka mixed with 1 teaspoon instant espresso, warmed

Loaf pan, approximately 22 x 12cm (9 x 5in), lined with baking parchment

1 Preheat the oven to 190°C/375°F/gas mark 5.

2 Sift the flour with the baking powder and set aside.

3 Put the chocolate in a small saucepan over a pan of simmering water and melt, stirring continuously. Stir in the vodka and set aside.

4 Blend the butter and sugar in a large mixing bowl. Then whisk in the eggs and *Vanilla Vodka*.

5 Gently fold the chocolate and vodka into the sugar and egg mixture.

6 Very slowly add a few spoonfuls of the flour to the chocolate mixture, stirring continuously. Then add a few spoonfuls of the boiling water. Continue to add flour and boiling water in this way until you have a smooth liquid batter.

7 Pour the batter into the lined loaf tin and bake for 25 minutes.

8 Reduce the oven temperature to 170°C/325°F/gas mark 3 and continue to bake for a further 20 minutes. (The cake should be firm to the touch but still jiggly in the middle. So don't fret if you insert a skewer and it doesn't emerge clean.)

9 Remove the tin from the oven and leave to cool on a rack (to allow cool air to pass beneath the tin and speed cooling) before you turn the loaf out of the tin.

10 While the loaf is cooling, make the *Espresso Vodka Glaze* by whisking together the icing sugar, salt and warm *Espresso Vodka*. Generously spread on the top and sides of loaf. Once the glaze sets, slice and serve.

VODKA CHOCOLATE MOUSSE

This recipe is dedicated to my brother Christopher (now a hot-shot attorney) who, at a very tender age, loved chocolate mousse so much he once marched into a restaurant kitchen to demand the chef's recipe (for our Mom to cook, of course). Chris, this one's for you.

Serves 6

4 eggs, separated

4 tablespoons sugar

4 tablespoons vodka

150g (5oz) milk chocolate, minimum 35 per cent cocoa solids, cut into small chunks

3 tablespoons strong freshly brewed coffee or espresso

75g (3oz) soft unsalted butter, cut into pieces

Vodka Whipped Cream (see page 119), to serve

Twisted Citrus (see page 119), to serve

1 Whisk the egg yolks and sugar in a large mixing bowl for 2–3 minutes, or until they are pale yellow and thick enough to form a ribbon when the whisk is lifted from the bowl.

2 Whisk in the vodka. Set the mixing bowl over a pan of simmering (not boiling) water, and continue to whisk for 3–4 minutes, or until the mixture is foamy and hot.

3 Set the bowl over a pan of iced water and whisk for a further 3–4 minutes, or until the mixture is cool, thick and creamy.

4 Place a medium, heavy-bottomed saucepan over another pan of simmering (not boiling) water. Add the chocolate and the coffee to the pan and stir constantly until the chocolate melts. Do not allow the chocolate to get too hot (or it may scorch) or allow it come into direct contact with the water or steam (or it may bind or clump).

5 When all of the chocolate has melted, whisk in the butter – one piece at a time – to make a smooth cream.

6 Slowly fold the chocolate mixture into the egg yolks and sugar.

7 Whisk the egg whites in a separate bowl until stiff peaks begin to form.

8 Stir about a quarter of the egg whites into the chocolate mixture to lighten it, then very gently fold in the remainder.

9 Spoon the mousse into martini glasses or dessert cups and refrigerate for at least 4 hours or until the mousse has set.

10 Serve with a dollop of *Vodka Whipped Cream* in each glass, and/or *Twisted Citrus* slices rolled in sugar.

SCREWDRIVER SOUFFLÉS

I was always intimidated by the prospect of cooking soufflés. I had visions of having to tiptoe around my oven for fear of the soufflé falling. But once I tried making one, I found that there's not all that much to it. Of course, I never tell my guests how simple they are to make; better that they continue to believe I'm a god in the kitchen.

Serves 8

25g (1oz) butter, softened

4 tablespoons icing sugar

4 egg yolks and 6 egg whites

110g (4oz) sugar

Grated zest and 4 tablespoons juice of
    1 orange

3 tablespoons *Orange Peel Vodka* (see
    page 142)

Vodka Orange Mandarin Sauce (see
    recipe below), warmed

1 Preheat the oven to 200°C/400°F/gas mark 6.

2 Lightly grease 8 small ramekins with butter; then dust with icing sugar (shaking away and reserving the excess).

3 Whisk the egg yolks with the sugar and orange zest until light and fluffy – about 3–4 minutes.

4 Add the orange juice and *Orange Peel Vodka* and whisk for 2–3 minutes until fully incorporated.

5 Whisk the egg whites in a separate bowl until stiff peaks form. Add about a spoonful of the egg whites to the orange mixture and stir in thoroughly. Very slowly fold the remainder of the egg whites into the orange mixture.

6 Spoon gently into the prepared ramekins, set them in a large roasting tin that contains about 3cm (1in) warm water and bake until the soufflés rise and turn golden brown – about 10 minutes.

7 Sift the remaining icing sugar on to the soufflés and serve immediately. At the table, poke a spoon into the top of each soufflé and spoon in warm *Vodka Orange Mandarin Sauce*.

When baking, have eggs and dairy ingredients at room temperature.

VODKA ORANGE MANDARIN SAUCE

Makes about 450ml (16fl oz)

225g (8oz) sugar

75g (3oz) unsalted butter, cut into pieces

4 tablespoons freshly squeezed orange juice

2 mandarin oranges, peeled and sectioned

3 large egg yolks, beaten

4 tablespoons *Orange Peel Vodka* (see
    page 142)

75ml (3fl oz) double cream

1 Combine the sugar, butter and orange juice in a small heavy saucepan held over another pan of simmering water. Whisk until the butter has melted and the sugar is completely incorporated. Add the mandarin oranges and cook until soft, stirring frequently – about 5–7 minutes.

2 Whisk in the egg yolks until thoroughly blended and cook for a further 2–3 minutes.

3 Whisk in the *Orange Peel Vodka* and cream and serve immediately (or let cool and refrigerate in an airtight container for up to 3 days; reheat on a low heat or over simmering water).

THE PIE THAT CAME IN FROM THE COLD

(Vodka Chocolate Icebox Pie)

My Mom often kept a chocolate icebox pie in our freezer hidden from sight lest I ruin my dinner. It was always a great treat when she would surprise me with her 'sans alcohol' version of this frozen pudding delight.

Since this pie and the vodka would occupy the same shelf in my freezer, I thought I might as well put them together. I have gone back to scratch on the recipe (Mom used instant pudding) and given it a little boost. But it still reminds me of days before colour TV.

Serves 6–8

2 tablespoons butter

400g (14oz) dark chocolate, minimum 70 per cent cocoa solids, in pieces

600ml (1 pint) cold milk

275g (10oz) sugar

250g (9oz) flour

½ teaspoon salt

4 tablespoons vodka

3 egg yolks, well beaten

2 teaspoons *Vanilla Vodka* (see page 143) or 1 teaspoon vanilla extract

600g (1¼lb) digestive biscuits, crushed

Vodka Whipped Cream (see opposite)

1 Combine the butter, chocolate and milk in a double boiler (or a mixing bowl over a pan of simmering water) and heat to melt. Whisk until blended.

2 Sift the sugar, flour and salt together. Add a small amount of the chocolate mixture to it and stir until blended well and the sugar dissolves. Add the vodka and stir. Combine the flour mix with mixture in double boiler and stir.

3 Slowly add a spoonful of this mixture to the egg yolks, while whisking vigorously to prevent the eggs from cooking. Once blended, add the egg yolks to the double boiler and stir.

4 When the mixture begins to thicken, remove from the heat, add the *Vanilla Vodka* and stir.

5 Layer the mixture into a buttered rectangular glass dish, alternating with layers of digestive biscuits and finishing with a layer of chocolate mixture.

6 Put the dish in the freezer overnight.

7 Cut into squares and serve – plain or topped with *Vodka Whipped Cream*.

VODKA WHIPPED CREAM

Always make whipped cream fresh. Don't even think about making this ahead of time or refrigerating it for future use. Vodka Whipped Cream makes a great topping for many of the desserts in this chapter. You can also give it a try on coffee drinks (or on an adventurous companion). Here are several flavour variations to mix and match with your favourite desserts.

VANILLA VODKA WHIPPED CREAM

Makes about 350ml (12fl oz)

225ml (8fl oz) whipping cream
2 tablespoons icing sugar
2 tablespoons *Vanilla Vodka* (see page 143)

1 Whip the cream until stiff in a large, chilled bowl.
2 Gradually stir in the sugar and vodka.

LEMON VODKA WHIPPED CREAM

Makes about 350ml (12fl oz)

225ml (8fl oz) whipping cream
2 tablespoons icing sugar
2 tablespoons *Lemon Peel Vodka* (see page 142)
2 teaspoons grated lemon zest

1 Whip the cream until stiff in a large, chilled bowl.
2 Gradually stir in the sugar, vodka and zest.

ORANGE VODKA WHIPPED CREAM

Makes about 350ml (12fl oz)

225ml (8fl oz) whipping cream
2 tablespoons icing sugar
2 tablespoons *Orange Peel Vodka* (see page 142)
2 teaspoons grated orange zest

1 Whip the cream until stiff in a large, chilled bowl.
2 Gradually stir in the sugar, vodka and zest.

TWISTED CITRUS

This is not technically a dessert. But with Twisted Citrus on hand, you have a colourful and tangy sweet decoration for any drink or treat.

Makes lots

12 oranges, lemons and/or limes, peel only, sliced into thin strips
350g (12oz) sugar
225ml (8fl oz) *Lemon Peel Vodka* (see page 142)

1 Put the peel in a saucepan, cover with water and simmer for about 30 minutes. Drain, cover again with water and simmer until tender – about 1 hour.
2 Combine the sugar with 350ml (12fl oz) water in a saucepan and stir over a low heat until the sugar completely dissolves.
3 Rinse and drain the peel and cook in the sugar syrup for about 1 hour. Cover and leave to cool – about 2–4 hours.
4 Drain and combine with the *Lemon Peel Vodka* in an airtight container and store in the fridge until needed. Use as is or rolled in sugar.

BLACK AND WHITE FLIGHTS

These sweet flights provide a great little finale to any meal. Even those who usually pass on dessert will find themselves raising these for one last sweet toast.

Makes 4

125ml (4fl oz) *Chocolate Walnut Vodka* (see page 146)

125ml (4fl oz) *Vodka Whipped Cream* (see page 119)

1 tablespoon chocolate shavings

1 Fill 4 chilled shot glasses with *Chocolate Walnut Vodka.*

2 Divide the *Vodka Whipped Cream* between the glasses and top with chocolate shavings.

BLITZED ICE CREAM

I ordered 'vodka ice cream' in a restaurant once. I was not impressed. It was just a few scoops of ice cream sitting in a puddle of vodka. That's not the way to do it. If you want the real deal, the vodka and ice cream have to be melded together. By blitzing the ice cream with the vodka and refreezing, you end up with a velvety-smooth concoction with a discernible tang. I favour this simple recipe – but feel free to experiment by combining different flavoured ice creams, infused vodkas and toppings (fruits, nuts, chocolate bits, etc).

Serves 4

600ml (1 pint) vanilla ice cream, softened

75ml (3fl oz) vodka or flavoured vodka (see Infusions, page 139)

Twisted Citrus (see page 119) or grated coconut, for topping

1 Whizz the ice cream and vodka in a blender or food-processor until well blended. Refreeze in an airtight container for 6–8 hours.

2 Scoop the ice cream mixture into chilled martini glasses and sprinkle with *Twisted Citrus* (see page 119), coconut or other topping.

ORANGE-BASIL VODKA SORBET

Basil doesn't often find its way into desserts. But it makes all the difference to this refreshing sorbet.

Serves 6–8

225ml (8fl oz) *Vodka Simple Syrup* (see page 129)

225ml (8fl oz) freshly squeezed orange juice (save the orange peel halves in your freezer until needed)

4 tablespoons vodka

⅛ teaspoon freshly squeezed lemon juice

6–8 large fresh basil leaves (and more for decoration, if desired)

Ice-cream maker

1 Put the *Vodka Simple Syrup* (it should be at room temperature) in a bowl and mix in the orange juice, vodka and lemon juice.

2 Bruise the basil leaves and steep in the mixture for about 1 hour.

3 Strain, place in the ice-cream maker and follow its instructions to produce sorbet.

4 Transfer the sorbet to the orange peel halves, decorate with a basil leaf and serve.

If you don't have an ice-cream maker, mix 600ml (1 pint) of melted orange sorbet with the basil, vodka and lemon juice. Let basil steep for about 1 hour then remove. Freeze the sorbet in the orange peel halves for about 3–4 hours and serve.

SIBERIAN ICE SQUARES

This is sort of a White Russian on a stick (ouch). A 'Russicle'?

Makes 12–16

300ml (½ pint) vanilla ice cream, softened

4 tablespoons chilled *Espresso Vodka* (see page 145) or vodka

4 tablespoons freshly brewed espresso, cooled

Ice lolly sticks or cocktail sticks

1 Whizz all the ingredients in a blender.

2 Fill an ice tray with the mixture and freeze for at least 24 hours.

3 Add the sticks when the mixture is slushy – after about 1 hour.

4 Carefully remove from the ice tray and serve 1–2 squares in shot glasses.

VODKA PANTRY

A little bit of planning and advance preparation can make cooking with vodka, and indeed cooking in general, easier and more enjoyable. A number of the recipes in this book rely upon the items in this chapter. They can all be stored in your pantry, fridge or freezer for weeks or months, so there's no reason not to make heaps (I store most condiments upside down in my fridge as this creates a virtually airtight seal that preserves the sauce for much longer). Add a few of the Infusions and Vodka Preserves to your collection and you'll be ready at a moment's notice to dazzle your guests (and yourself) with many of the distilled delectables in this book.

KGB SAUCE

I'm a 'chilli head' from way back. I like to pour on the heat every once in a while. But there isn't much choice of hot sauces in Moscow. And I like the idea of making my own concoction – using vodka, of course. That's how KGB Sauce was born. The heat in this sauce, much like the former KGB, sneaks up on you.

You will find that I use this sauce to introduce heat and an extra kick to a great many of the recipes in this book.

Makes about 350ml (12fl oz)

300g (10½oz) thick-skinned red chillies
   (Dutch or hot Anaheim)

3 garlic cloves, unpeeled

3 tablespoons extra-virgin olive oil

75g (3oz) onions, finely chopped

75g (3oz) tomatoes, finely chopped

2 teaspoons sugar

1 tablespoon freshly squeezed lemon juice

4 tablespoons vodka

½ teaspoon salt

¼ teaspoon freshly ground black pepper

1 Preheat the oven to 150°C/300°F/gas mark 2.

2 Slice the chillies in half lengthways from stem to tip. Remove the stems, seeds and membranes.

3 Arrange the chillies – cut-side down – in a roasting tin. Add the garlic, drizzle with olive oil and place in the centre of the oven until the skins blacken and blister – about 15–20 minutes. Leave to cool.

4 Strip away the blackened skins from the chillies with a paring knife and pop the garlic cloves out of their skins.

5 Heat the skinned chillies and garlic in a medium sauté pan over a moderate heat, stir in the onions, tomatoes and sugar and cook for about 5 minutes. Then add the lemon juice, vodka, salt and pepper. Stir for about 1 minute longer, then remove from the heat.

6 Transfer the chilli mixture to a blender or food-processor and whizz to a smooth purée. KGB Sauce will keep in the fridge in an airtight container for several months.

To get more juice from a lemon or lime, roll (while applying pressure) on a work surface, then microwave on high for about 20 seconds before cutting and squeezing it.

Wear rubber gloves when handling hot chillies. And wash your hands thoroughly with soap and water before bringing them into contact with eyes or other sensitive body parts. You have been warned.

Another trick for handling hot chillies is to coat your fingers in cooking oil before they are exposed to the chillies. This will act as a barrier to reduce the amount of capsaicin (the hot stuff in peppers) that enters the pores. It should just rinse away with the oil when you wash your hands.

VODKA AND ONION KETCHUP

Ketchup does not always have to come out of a bottle. And it does not always have to feature tomatoes. There are all different kinds of ketchup or 'catsup'. This one features vodka and caramelised onions. Use it the same way you would the bottled stuff. It's also a great wet rub for meats, and it can stand in well as a BBQ sauce. Fire it up by adding extra KGB Sauce.

Makes about 850ml (1½ pints)

5 tablespoons olive oil

5 large red onions, thinly sliced

4 tablespoons crushed garlic

1 tablespoon very finely chopped fresh
  ginger

1 medium tomato, finely chopped

2 teaspoons *KGB Sauce* (see page 124)
  or hot red pepper sauce

5 tablespoons Worcestershire sauce

125ml (4fl oz) molasses

125ml (4fl oz) cider vinegar

5 tablespoons vodka

2 tablespoons fresh lemon juice

1 teaspoon ground allspice

Salt and freshly ground black pepper,
  to taste

1 Heat the oil in a large, heavy-bottomed frying pan over a moderate heat.

2 Add the onions and cook until caramelised (well-browned) – about 30 minutes.

3 Add the garlic, ginger and tomato. Cook until the tomato softens – about 3 minutes.

4 Add the *KGB Sauce*, Worcestershire sauce, molasses, cider vinegar, vodka, lemon juice and allspice.

5 Lower the heat and reduce the mixture until it thickens, stirring frequently – about 15 minutes.

6 Remove from the heat and leave to cool to room temperature. Season with salt and pepper.

7 Once cool, whizz in a blender or food-processor to a smooth purée. Vodka and Onion Ketchup will keep, covered and refrigerated, for up to 30 days.

VODKA CHICKEN BROTH

Stock cubes are too salty. Tinned stocks and broths are convenient, but thin on flavour. So please, please do yourself a favour and prepare your own from scratch. Once I discovered how easy they are to make I vowed never to go back to shop-bought.

I know I am oversimplifying when I say that there is not much difference between broth, stock and consommé. They're all made in much the same way – though bones are not required for a broth (which is basically anything boiled). But while stock is primarily a foundation for other dishes, and consommé is essentially stock or broth cooked down and otherwise fussed over, broth is quicker to prepare and is also considered a soup in its own right. This makes it far more practical and versatile for the home cook, in my humble opinion.

This broth (and the Vodka Beef Broth that follows), with vodka and a hint of ginger, is very satisfying on its own or with some rice or noodles. And it will add a sweetness, flavour and complexity to many dishes. Since I use it in numerous recipes, I keep some in my freezer at all times.

Makes about 1 litre (1¾ pints)

1 whole chicken, skinned

2 small carrots

2 medium onions, with some skin on, rinsed

1 celery stick

2.5cm (1in) piece of fresh ginger, peeled

2 bay leaves

8 black peppercorns

225ml (8fl oz) *Basil Vodka* (see page 146) or vodka

6 basil leaves

Salt

1 Put the first 6 ingredients in a large stockpot or saucepan with enough very cold water to cover.

2 Slowly bring the stockpot to the boil over a moderate heat. Immediately reduce the heat to low, cover, and simmer for 1–1½ hours, skimming the fat from the surface four or five times while cooking.

3 Add the peppercorns, *Basil Vodka* and basil leaves and continue to simmer for 10 minutes.

4 Strain the broth. Add salt to taste and use in your favourite recipe. Or leave to cool to room temperature and store in an airtight container in the fridge or freezer.

The boiled chicken meat can be boned, shredded and returned to the broth for a simple and delicious chicken soup.

VODKA BEEF BROTH

This is an equally full-flavoured broth, useful in making hearty sauces, soups and other dishes.

Makes about 1 litre (1¾ pints)

450g (1lb) beef on the bone
2 small carrots
2 onions, with some skin on, rinsed
1 celery stick
2.5 cm (1in) piece of fresh ginger, peeled
2 bay leaves
8 black peppercorns
225ml (8fl oz) vodka
3 tablespoons freshly chopped parsley
Salt

1 Place the first 6 ingredients in a stockpot or saucepan with enough very cold water to cover.

2 Slowly bring the stockpot to the boil over a moderate heat. Immediately reduce the heat to low, cover, and simmer for 2–2½ hours, skimming the fat from the surface four or five times while cooking.

3 Add the peppercorns, vodka and parsley and continue to simmer for 10–15 minutes

4 Strain the broth. Add salt to taste and use in your favourite recipe. Or leave to cool to room temperature and store in an airtight container in the fridge or freezer.

For a darker, richer broth, roast the beef, bones and vegetables for about 30 minutes in an oven preheated to 230°C/450°F/gas mark 8, before adding them to your stockpot with water.

The best way to remove the fat and protein that collects on the surface of broths is to use a skimmer (which skims away debris using a flat mesh screen) or a 'fat mop' (fat adheres to its plastic mop).

You can freeze *Vodka Chicken Broth* or *Vodka Beef Broth* in ice cube trays. Then transfer the frozen cubes to a re-sealable bag or container. When ready to use, simply defrost as many cubes as you need in a microwave.

MOSCOW FRY BREAD

Here is my version of this Native American bread. I use it to make several of the recipes in this book, like Martini Pizzetta Flambé (see page 30) or Moscow Tacos (see page 76). It's also quite good simply drizzled with honey or toasted and served with dip or salsa, or as you might use any tortilla or flatbread.

Makes 20 or more rounds

500g (18oz) flour, plus extra for dusting

2 teaspoons salt

2 teaspoons baking powder

125ml (4fl oz) still mineral water

4 tablespoons vodka

225ml (8fl oz) warm milk

1 tablespoon sugar

225ml (8fl oz) vegetable oil

1 Sift together the flour, salt and baking powder into a large bowl.

2 Add the water, vodka, milk and sugar to the flour mixture. Since protein levels in flour vary by brand, use more or less flour or water as necessary until a sticky dough is formed.

3 Transfer the dough to a work surface dusted with additional flour and knead by repeatedly folding and pressing the dough with your hands into the surface. Roll it into a ball, cover in cling film and leave to rest for about 15 minutes.

4 Pinch off a small piece of dough (about the size of a golf ball) and roll into a small ball. Using a rolling pin and plenty of flour, roll each ball into a circle about 18cm (7in) in diameter. You may need to experiment with the size and thickness of the bread by starting with more or less dough.

5 Heat about 1 tablespoon of oil in a medium heavy-bottomed frying pan over a moderate-high heat. Drop a dough circle into the middle of the pan and give the pan a gentle shake to ensure the dough doesn't stick to the pan. Fry for about 10–20 seconds (depending on thickness), or until the underside begins to turn golden brown. Flip and cook until both sides are golden brown and transfer to a covered platter. Add more oil as necessary and repeat until all the dough is used.

You can spice up this recipe by adding about 1 tablespoon of chopped fresh herbs or dried fruit or 1 teaspoon of dried herbs (rosemary, basil or oregano) or freshly ground black pepper to the flour mixture before adding the milk, vodka and water. Or try adding 1 tablespoon of finely chopped jalapeño chillies, crushed garlic or sweetcorn to the warm milk before adding to the flour mixture.

Rolled dough or cooked bread can be placed between sheets of wax paper or foil in a sealed container and frozen for several weeks.

ROASTED PEPPER SALSA À LA VODKA

Roasting the peppers and tomatoes gives this salsa its smoky flavour. Serve it as a topping, as a dip for toasted wedges of Moscow Fry Bread (see page 128), or to accompany Moscow Tacos (see page 76). If you want a milder salsa, omit or use less KGB Sauce.

Makes about 450ml (16fl oz)

1 red pepper, quartered and de-seeded

3 large plum tomatoes, halved and de-seeded

1 jalapeño chilli, halved and de-seeded

1 tablespoon extra-virgin olive oil

Salt and freshly ground black pepper, to taste

½ teaspoon *KGB Sauce* (see page 124; optional)

1 tablespoon chopped spring onions

1 tablespoon fresh lime juice

2 tablespoons vodka

1 Preheat the grill to hot. Put the pepper, tomatoes and jalapeño – cut-side up – in a medium roasting tin. Drizzle with oil and season with salt and pepper. Place the tin under the grill for about 15 minutes.

2 Remove the tin from the grill and combine the peppers and tomatoes with the remaining ingredients in a blender or food processor and pulse quickly a few times. Do not purée as you want a chunky salsa.

VODKA SIMPLE SYRUP

Sugar is slow to dissolve – especially in cold foods or drinks, so Vodka Simple Syrup to the rescue.

Makes about 450ml (16fl oz)

325ml (11fl oz) still mineral water

900g (2lb) granulated sugar

125ml (4fl oz) vodka

1 Bring the water to the boil in a large saucepan. Reduce the heat to moderate, add the sugar and stir until it dissolves completely.

2 Reduce the heat to low and simmer for 10 minutes until the mixture has a syrup consistency.

3 Add the vodka, mix well and cool.

4 Transfer to a jar or container and reserve for use.

(The recipe can be doubled or trebled as necessary.)

In a tightly sealed container, Vodka Simple Syrup keeps indefinitely – though it may begin to crystallise over time. If it crystallises, simply warm the container in a saucepan of slow-simmering water.

STILL ART

To guarantee outstanding purity, every drop of Smirnoff No. 21 vodka is filtered 10 times through natural hardwood charcoal, a process which takes a full 8 hours.

That's right. Chutneys and jams can all benefit from the addition of vodka. And although the whole idea of preserves may conjure up images of dear old granny surrounded by bubbling pots and a sticky cache of jam jars, they are surprisingly simple to make. What's more, if stored with care, they can be kept in your pantry, fridge or freezer for a good long while – ready and waiting to be used as toppings, spreads for toasts or biscuits, or to introduce concentrated flavours into your favourite dishes.

PRESERVES

VODKA APRICOT CHUTNEY

You will welcome a dollop of this chutney with your favourite savoury or spicy snack.

Makes about 450ml (16fl oz)

1 tablespoon vegetable oil

225g (8oz) onions, chopped

1 tablespoon finely chopped fresh ginger

4 tablespoons vodka

1 tablespoon mustard seeds

1 teaspoon curry powder

⅛ teaspoon cayenne pepper

450g (1lb) dried apricots, chopped

175g (6oz) sultanas

125ml (4fl oz) white wine vinegar

75g (3oz) granulated sugar

Salt, to taste

60g (2½oz) chopped fresh coriander

1 Heat the oil in a medium non-stick heavy-bottomed frying pan and sauté the onions and ginger until the onions are lightly browned – about 4–6 minutes.

2 Add the vodka and, stirring constantly, mix in the mustard seeds, curry powder and cayenne pepper and cook for about 4 minutes.

3 Mix in the apricots, sultanas, vinegar and sugar and cook for about 7 minutes.

4 Stir in the salt and coriander, remove from the heat and leave to cool. Serve chilled or at room temperature.

Vodka Apricot Chutney will keep in your fridge in an airtight container for several weeks.

VODKA APPLE MAPLE JAM

I like to spread this one on corn muffins. But you can spread it anywhere you like. It's your jam.

Makes about 2 litres (3½ pints)

2.25kg (5lb) apples, peeled, cored and finely chopped

225ml (8fl oz) maple syrup

1 teaspoon ground cinnamon

½ teaspoon ground allspice

½ teaspoon grated nutmeg

¼ teaspoon cloves

125ml (4fl oz) still mineral water

1.3kg (3lb) sugar

125ml (4fl oz) vodka

1 Combine the apples, maple syrup and spices with the mineral water in a large saucepan. Bring slowly to the boil over a moderate heat.

2 Reduce the heat to low, add the sugar and simmer until syrupy – about 1 hour – stirring frequently.

3 Turn off the heat, stir in the vodka and leave to stand for about 5 minutes before pouring into warm sterilised jars.

There are traditional ways of sterilising jars by boiling or by heating in the oven. But the simplest way is to use jars and lids hot from the dishwasher. Pour the hot jam into the warm jars, tighten the lids and immediately turn them upside down. You can turn them back the right way up once they cool and then store them for use.

For long-term non-refrigerated storage, soak the filled jars in a boiling-water bath for 5 minutes immediately after sealing them. Leave to cool and store.

VODKA APRICOT DATE JAM

This jam is put to good use in my Glazed and Confused Chicken (see page 63). But I confess that I sometimes eat this one right out of the jar. Just a few spoonfuls with my tea. Is that so wrong?

Makes about 600ml (1 pint)

225g (8oz) dried apricot halves, stoned

225g (8oz) dates, pitted

350ml (12fl oz) still mineral water

Juice and grated zest of 1 orange

60g (2½oz) sugar

½ teaspoon almond extract

4 tablespoons *Orange Peel Vodka* (see page 142)

1 Combine the apricots, dates and mineral water in a medium bowl, cover and leave to stand overnight or until soft and plump – about 12 hours.

2 Transfer to a large saucepan with the orange juice and zest and simmer for 5 minutes.

3 Add the sugar and bring to the boil, stirring frequently, until the mixture is thick and shiny – about 45 minutes.

4 Turn off the heat, stir in the almond extract and *Orange Peel Vodka* and let stand for about 5 minutes before pouring into warm sterilised jars.

SWEET ONION VODKA JAM

I once (OK, twice) found myself spreading this jam on a sausage roll at 2am. And I'm man enough to admit it.

Makes about 1 litre (1¾ pints)
40g (1½oz) butter
2 teaspoons extra-virgin olive oil
6 onions, thinly sliced
½ teaspoon salt
75g (3oz) dark brown sugar
4 tablespoons vodka

1 Melt the butter and oil in heavy-bottomed frying pan over a moderate-high heat. Add the onions and sauté until slightly brown – about 15 minutes. Season with salt. Reduce the heat, stirring constantly until the onions are caramel coloured and very tender (they will reduce considerably in size) – about 30 minutes. Add the brown sugar and stir until dissolved. Stir in the vodka and mix until it is completely absorbed by the onion mixture.
2 Put in warm sterilised jars and refrigerate until ready to serve on bread or biscuits. It may also be re-heated and served with meat, chicken or turkey.

VODKA PEPPER JAM

This sweet and fiery jam can be addictive when spread on crackers, used as a dip for tortilla chips, or as a topping on sliced meats in sandwiches.

Makes 700ml (1¼ pints)
1 tablespoon extra-virgin olive oil
225g (8oz) onions, finely chopped
500g (18oz) hot red chillies, finely chopped
225g (8oz) red peppers, de-seeded and finely chopped
225g (8oz) tomatoes, de-seeded and finely chopped
225ml (8fl oz) honey
125ml (4fl oz) fresh lemon juice
125ml (4fl oz) vodka

1 Warm the oil in a medium saucepan over a moderate heat. Add the onions, the hot chillies and red peppers and tomatoes and cook until very soft – about 15–20 minutes.
2 Add the honey and lemon juice and simmer until very thick and syrupy – about 10 minutes – stirring occasionally.
3 Turn off the heat, stir in the vodka and leave to stand for about 5 minutes before pouring into warm sterilised jars.

STRAWBERRY VODKA JAM

Spread this on anything (or anyone), or pulse a few times with creamy yogurt.

Makes about 850ml (1½ pints)
500g (18oz) strawberries, washed and hulled
1 green apple, peeled, cored and finely chopped
3 tablespoons freshly squeezed lime juice
125ml (4fl oz) still mineral water
175g (6oz) sugar
4 tablespoons *Orange Peel Vodka* (see page 142)

1 Combine the strawberries, apple and lime juice in a large saucepan with the mineral water and leave to stand, covered, for 30 minutes.
2 Bring the pan to the boil over a moderate heat while stirring.
3 Reduce the heat to low, add the sugar and simmer until syrupy – about 1 hour – stirring every 10 minutes.
4 Turn off the heat, stir in the *Orange Peel Vodka* and leave to stand for about 5 minutes before pouring into warm sterilised jars.

RASPBERRY VODKA JAM

This jam whispers to me every time I have pancakes.

1 Combine the raspberries, apple and lemon juice in a large saucepan with the mineral water and leave to stand, covered, for 30 minutes.

2 Bring the pan to the boil over a moderate heat while stirring.

3 Reduce the heat to low, add the sugar and simmer until syrupy – about 1 hour – stirring every 10 minutes.

4 Turn off the heat, stir in the *Orange Peel Vodka* and leave to stand for about 5 minutes before pouring into warm sterilised jars.

Makes about 450ml (16fl oz)

1kg (2lb) raspberries

1 green apple, peeled, cored and finely chopped

4 tablespoons freshly squeezed lemon juice

125ml (4fl oz) still mineral water

175g (6oz) sugar

4 tablespoons *Lemon Peel Vodka* (see page 142)

INFUSIONS

OK, here it is: the real secret to creating wonderfully unique vodka dishes and drinks. B[y] taking the time to prepare your own vodka infusions you are, in essence, concocting you[r] own secret ingredients. By crafting custom-infused vodkas, you can introduce distinct flavour[s] to your dishes, which would otherwise be difficult to reproduce. On their own (chilled or ove[r] ice) or in cocktails, many infusions make wonderful drinks and truly novel gifts.

Flavouring vodka is a near-ancient tradition – not just the latest marketing idea fro[m] modern distillers. Two hundred years ago every nobleman or member of the gentry i[n] Russia and other parts of Eastern Europe produced his own vodka, often infused with fruits berries, grains, herbs and spices for flavour – or to mask impurities.

A quick Russian lesson: Nastoika is the name Russians have given to all infuse[d] vodkas. The popular 'sweet infusions' are called Nalivka, meaning any beverage made b[y] stewing or macerating different fruits and berries in vodka (sometimes for many months) The most popular Nalivka is Vishnyovka, sour cherry vodka.

A favourite Nastoika would often be prepared to mark a special occasion, holiday, even[t] or visit. I have even heard of one very old tradition where an honoured guest may be serve[d] a selection of specially prepared vodkas – with the first letter of each vodka flavour spelling the name of the honoree. I guess they must have had a lot more time on their hands back then

Most important of all, please remember that you will achieve the best results using the highest-quality ingredients. That includes the vodka.

You will find a number of different infusion techniques and helpful hints in the recipes that follow. But here are the four basic steps:

1. CHOOSE WHAT YOU INFUSE.

There are two ways to add flavour to vodka. You can mix flavour extracts and concentrates directly into the vodka. Or, you can steep raw ingredients in vodka long enough to allow the flavours to slowly penetrate and infuse the vodka. In my experience, the best results, greatest control and most number of combinations can generally be achieved through the infusion method. And if the infusion turns out too strong, just dilute it with more vodka to achieve the desired strength.

Whole fruit should be sliced, mashed or 'bruised' in order to encourage the juices to escape and allow the vodka to macerate the fruit thoroughly. Just as in wine-making, leave the skins on to impart the full flavour and richness of the fruit. And experiment with different ripeness of fruits to explore various intensities of flavour. The easiest and most economical way to choose your flavouring ingredients is to select fruits most abundant in your area at the time of year you choose to create your infusion. When in season, my pal Gary Kenner would buy baskets of raspberries from New England markets and treat us all to his tasty infusion several weeks later.

Virtually any fresh or dried fruit, berry, herb, spice or flavouring can be infused into vodka. Many of the recipes in this book call for vodka infused with lemons or oranges, basil, apples, vanilla pods, hot chillies or espresso coffee. But you might also try lemongrass, cinnamon sticks, nutmeg, dill, tarragon or rosemary. I have even read about infusions made with jellybeans and candy bars. You are limited only by your imagination.

You can also combine any number of ingredients to create flavours that range from the traditional – like apple-cinnamon – to the truly unique. Chilli/garlic/basil anyone? What's more, you can even blend vodkas after they have been infused. For example, you can blend a lemon-infusion with an

2. MIX IT UP.

Once you have chosen your flavourings, you need to combine them with vodka (or vodka and sugar) in any glass or earthenware jar or jug with a tight-fitting lid. Then just put the container in a dark, dry place (for example, a kitchen cabinet) and leave it at room temperature for as long as desired. Most fruits need several weeks or months for all their flavour to be infused into the vodka. (I generally find that the riper the fruit, the less time will be required for the infusion.) However, chillies, garlic and most fresh spices may need only a couple of days. If you are uncertain as to how long an infusion may take, I suggest you taste your vodka daily until you achieve the desired effect. It's for science, after all!

If you are making a sweet infusion, never add sugar directly to the vodka because the sugar may not completely dissolve. Instead, you can introduce the sugar in one of two ways. You can combine your mashed fruit and sugar before you add the vodka, allowing the sugar and fruit to thoroughly combine and ferment. Or, you can combine two parts sugar to one part water in a pan over moderate heat until the sugar completely dissolves and a thick syrup results (or use Vodka Simple Syrup, see page 129). Let the syrup cool and then combine it with your infused vodka for the desired sweetness.

3. NO STRAIN NO GAIN.

You will need to strain any bits of fruit, leaf or sediment from your vodka by slowly decanting it through a coffee filter or piece of wet muslin or cheesecloth. Depending on how long fruits have been in the vodka, you may find they can be added to sugar and puréed into a topping or jam. But in most cases the flavour will be completely consumed by the vodka.

4. PUT A CORK IT.

And make some friends. Infused vodkas make memorable presents in a world where few people seem to craft anything themselves any more. Small bottles are great parting gifts for dinner guests. And larger bottles make for unique holiday or housewarming gifts. Take a bottle of infused vodka to your next dinner party. Anyone can buy a decent bottle of Chablis. But your host will be thrilled with a decorative bottle of home-made vodka infusion.

Any glass bottle with a tight-fitting stopper or cork will do the trick. Garnish your bottles with a small quantity or sprig of its key ingredient when appropriate. And a custom label and/or a fancy ribbon or string tied around its neck will dress it up for gift-giving. (Of course, a copy of this book would make a fine accessory to any infusion.)

Anyway, go infuse yourself.

ORANGE PEEL VODKA

Two of the most commonly available commercial infusions are with orange or lemon. So you may choose to purchase them at your local off-licence. But I encourage you to make your own and experiment with the intensity of the citrus flavour by varying the duration of the infusion or amount of citrus peel.

3 large oranges
1 litre (1¾ pints) vodka

1 Wash the oranges. Using a zester or vegetable peeler, peel the skin to create narrow ribbons. Scrape away any remaining pith.
2 Put the peel into a large jar and add the vodka. Store in a dark, dry place for about 2 weeks, shaking the jar occasionally.
3 Strain through wet muslin or cheesecloth, discard the peel and store in a bottle ready for use.

LEMON PEEL VODKA

I rely on this infusion when I want to add a hint of citrus to drinks and foods.

4 lemons
1 litre (1¾ pints) vodka

1 Wash the lemons. Using a zester or vegetable peeler, peel the skin to create narrow ribbons. Scrape away any remaining pith.
2 Put the peel into a large jar and add the vodka. Store in a dark, dry place for about 2 weeks, shaking the jar occasionally.
3 Strain through wet muslin or cheesecloth, discard the peel and store in a bottle ready for use.

LIMONCELLO

OK, so it's not exactly the limoncello you find in Italy where the lemons grown in Sicily or along the Amalfi Coast provide an exquisitely balanced sweet/tart flavour. But this lemon vodka recipe comes real close. Serve it the way the Italians do – as a chilled digestive after a hearty meal.

5 lemons
1 orange
1 litre (1¾ pints) vodka
225ml (8fl oz) fresh lemon juice
600ml (1 pint) *Vodka Simple Syrup* (see page 129)

1 Wash the fruit. Using a zester or vegetable peeler, peel the skin to create narrow ribbons. Scrape away any remaining pith.
2 Put the peel and lemon juice into a large jar and add the vodka. Store in a dark, dry place for about 2 weeks.
3 Add the *Vodka Simple Syrup* to the vodka mixture, strain through wet muslin or cheesecloth and store in a bottle ready for use. Chill in the fridge until ready to serve.

RASPBERRY VODKA

I would be hard-pressed to find a more refreshing cocktail than this Raspberry Vodka with lime juice poured over ice.

1.8 litres (3 pints) red raspberries
1 litre (1¾ pints) vodka
225ml (8fl oz) *Vodka Simple Syrup* (see page 129)

1 Put the raspberries into a large, shallow dish and mash with a fork or potato masher.
2 Transfer the fruit and juice to a large glass jar and cover with the vodka. Seal the jar, shake to blend, and set it aside in a dark, dry place for about 6 weeks. Give it a shake every week or so.
3 Strain the contents of the jar through a fine sieve into a large glass bowl. Discard the fruit, rinse the sieve and the jar thoroughly. Fit the sieve with a damp coffee filter, or a double layer of kitchen paper, and strain the flavoured vodka back into the jar.
4 Add the *Vodka Simple Syrup* to the vodka mixture. Reseal the jar and shake gently to blend. Then transfer to a bottle and store for 2–3 days before serving.

APPLE VODKA

In this recipe, the sugar is added to the fruit and allowed to ferment for about a week to accentuate the apple flavour before adding vodka. Apple vodka is delicious over ice. And it is surprisingly versatile for cooking.

3 apples
225g (8oz) sugar
1 cinnamon stick
1 litre (1¾ pints) vodka

1 Wash and core the apples and cut into small pieces. Place in a large jar with the sugar and seal. Store for 3–5 days.
2 Add the cinnamon and vodka and re-seal. Shake to blend the ingredients and store in a dark, dry place for about 1 week, shaking the jar every few days.
3 Strain the mixture through wet muslin or cheesecloth and store in a bottle ready for use.

If the result is too sweet for your taste, dilute with more vodka.

VANILLA VODKA

While not quite as concentrated as commercially available extract, this version has a natural, fuller flavour and is a great addition to coffees and desserts. I like to add a few teaspoons to Coca-Cola over ice. It beats the pants off the version found in shops. Use it full-strength for the recipes in this book or dilute with more vodka to achieve a subtle, ready-to-drink variation.

5 vanilla pods
500ml (18fl oz) vodka

1 Split the vanilla pods lengthways down the centre to expose the seeds, keeping the pods of the beans intact.
2 Place the pods with the vodka in a large jar with an airtight seal. Store in a dark, dry place for at least 4 weeks, shaking the jar several times each week.
3 When ready, transfer the extract and the pods to a bottle. As you use the extract, top off with more vodka to replenish your supply. The pods will continue to impart flavour for many months.

ESPRESSO VODKA

The result of this infusion will be akin to a strong, sweet coffee liqueur. Use it to make White Russians or on its own over ice, poured over ice cream, or added to coffee.

225ml (8fl oz) freshly brewed espresso
450g (1lb) sugar
500ml (18fl oz) vodka
1 teaspoon *Vanilla Vodka* (see page 143), vanilla extract or 1 whole vanilla pod

1 Heat the espresso in a medium saucepan over a moderate heat and slowly add the sugar, stirring constantly, until it has completely dissolved. Leave to cool.
2 Add the vodka and *Vanilla Vodka* or vanilla extract (if using) and stir.
3 Pour the mixture into a large jar and store in a dark, dry place for at least 48 hours. (If using a whole vanilla pod, add it to the jar before pouring in the mixture and remove it when you achieve the desired flavour intensity.)
4 Strain the mixture into a decorative bottle or two and store ready for use.

I use my prized espresso machine and a quality Italian brand of espresso. If you don't have an espresso maker at home, buy a large cup of strong espresso at your nearest café. If you use filter coffee or instant you may lose your place in heaven.

CHILLI VODKA

Burn baby, burn.

225g (8oz) whole chillies (such as jalapeño, habañero or poblano)
1 litre (1¾ pints) vodka

1 Wash and dry the chillies and slit them lengthways into slivers (for less heat, remove the seeds). Place in a large jar with the vodka and infuse for 7–10 days in a dark, dry place.
2 Strain the mixture through wet muslin or cheesecloth and store in a bottle ready for use in martinis or other cocktails.

PINEAPPLE VODKA

Pineapple vodka was among my Mom's favourite drinks. We used to frequent a well-known Boston eatery where they would keep an enormous glass vat on the bar filled with pineapple and Russian vodka. They would simply strain the pineapple vodka over ice into a martini glass with a pineapple wedge as a garnish. Cheers, Mom!

450g (1lb) fresh pineapple, trimmed and chopped
1 litre (1¾ pints) vodka
4 tablespoons *Vodka Simple Syrup* (see page 129; optional)

1 Put the fruit in a large airtight jar.
2 Pour in the vodka (and *Vodka Simple Syrup* if you like it sweet). Seal the jar and store in a dark, dry place for about 2 weeks.
3 Strain through a wet muslin or cheesecloth into a bottle ready for use.

CHOCOLATE WALNUT VODKA

Here's another bottled dessert. Serve over ice or pour over ice cream.

225g (8oz) milk chocolate, minimum 35 per cent cocoa solids
4 tablespoons freshly brewed espresso or coffee
225g (8oz) granulated sugar
110g (4oz) walnuts, chopped
1 teaspoon *Vanilla Vodka* (see page 143) or vanilla extract
1.5 litres (2½ pints) vodka

1 Melt the chocolate with the espresso in a small saucepan held over a pan of simmering water.
2 Slowly whisk in the sugar and mix until it has completely dissolved into the chocolate mixture.
3 Pour the mixture into a large jar, add the walnuts, *Vanilla Vodka* and vodka, shake and seal. Store in a dark, dry place for 48 hours, shaking the jar several times each day.
4 Shake well and strain through a fine sieve into a bottle ready for use. Discard the walnuts. Shake the bottle vigorously before each use.

SOUR CHERRY VODKA (*Vishnyovka*)

This is among the most common home infusions in Russia. Once again, the fruit and sugar are combined to begin a fermentation process before the vodka is added.

900g (2lb) sour cherries, fresh or frozen and defrosted, stoned
250g (8oz) sugar
1 teaspoon ground cinnamon
½ teaspoon grated nutmeg
1 litre (1¾ pints) vodka

1 Rinse and crush the cherries. Place in a large jar with the sugar, cinnamon and nutmeg. Seal the jar and store for 3–5 days.
2 Add the vodka, reseal and shake well. Store for 5 days in a dark, dry place.
3 Strain the *Vishnyovka* through wet muslin or cheesecloth into a bottle ready for use.

If the result is too sweet for your taste, dilute with more vodka.

BASIL VODKA

Basil vodka is perfect for cooking – particularly in sauces and recipes using tomatoes. Combine it with plain vodka in your favourite Bloody Mary recipe (see Bloody Natasha, see page 151). Or mix it evenly with oil and vinegar, then toss with greens and vegetables for a vodka-inspired salad dressing.

12 large basil leaves
500ml (18fl oz) vodka
Sprig of basil to decorate

1 Wash and dry the basil leaves and combine with about a third of the vodka in a small bowl. Use a wooden spoon to stir and bruise the leaves to release their natural oils and flavour.
2 Add this mixture to the remainder of the vodka and store in an airtight container for about 24–48 hours in a dark, dry place. Stir or shake several times to circulate the leaves.
3 Strain through wet muslin or cheesecloth into a bottle and store or display, ready for use.

DRINKS

This is by no means an exhaustive list of vodka drinks. There are many very fine cocktail books available – including a few devoted exclusively to vodka. And, as I have explained elsewhere in this book, most Russians and vodka purists rarely mix anything with their favourite spirit. There is one exception to this rule. Many Russians drink vodka with beer, or pour vodka into beer – the Russian equivalent to a Boilermaker (a shot of Scotch or Bourbon dropped into a mug of beer). A common Russian expression is 'Vodka without beer is your money wasted!'

But what's a book about vodka without a few vodka cocktails and drinks? So here are a few potions you may not find in the average bar book. Several of these drinks recipes rely upon flavoured vodkas -- all of which appear in Infusions. Na Zdorovie.

BLUE MARTINI

I'm a fan of Smirnoff's Norsk vodka.
It is delicately flavoured with Nordic
berries and has an icy blue colour.
Chilled and married with a hint of
vanilla, it makes for a cool blue
cocktail.

Makes 4 (3 units per glass)
300ml (10fl oz) Smirnoff Norsk Vodka
1 teaspoon *Vanilla Vodka* (see page 143)
   or ½ teaspoon vanilla extract
Coffee beans or fresh blueberries,
   to garnish

1 Shake the Norsk Vodka and
Vanilla Vodka over ice and strain
into a large martini glass,
garnished with a few coffee beans
or blueberries.

BLOODY NATASHA

I have tasted a lot of truly horrible Bloody Marys over the years. Most were too watery; many lacked flavour or any kind of spicy punch. But with a little extra effort (OK... a lot of extra effort) I found I could prepare the rich, thick eye-opener I craved. Now you can too.

Makes 4 (2 units per glass)

4 tomatoes, halved

1 whole jalapeño chilli, halved

1 tablespoon olive oil

Salt and freshly ground black pepper,
     to taste

2 tablespoons freshly grated horseradish

2 tablespoons fresh lemon juice

1 tablespoon fresh lime juice

2 tablespoons Worcestershire sauce

1 teaspoon celery salt

½ teaspoon sugar

½ teaspoon *KGB Sauce* (see page 124)
     or hot red pepper sauce (optional)

200ml (7fl oz) *Basil Vodka* (see
     page 146) or vodka

2 lime wedges to decorate

2 celery sticks, to decorate

2 whole jalapeños chillies, to decorate

1 Preheat the oven to 180°C/350°F/gas mark 4.

2 Place the tomatoes and jalapeños in a medium roasting tin – cut-side up. Drizzle with the olive oil and season with salt and pepper. Bake until the skins begin to blacken and the flesh to soften – about 20 minutes.

3 Transfer to a blender or food-processor with the horseradish, lemon juice, lime juice, Worcestershire sauce, celery salt, sugar and black pepper to taste. If you like, add the *KGB Sauce* for additional heat. Whizz to desired consistency. Chill in the fridge until needed.

4 When ready to serve, run the lime wedges around the rim of a tall chilled glass. Then turn the moistened rim in a shallow dish containing a mixture of salt and pepper. Add a celery stick, ice and 50ml (2fl oz) of vodka. Fill the glass with the chilled tomato mixture. Finally skewer a lime wedge and jalapeño with a cocktail stick and stab into the celery stick. Serve with a wink and a smile.

VODKA SANGRIA

A Spanish punch thrown with a Russian hook. Serve this at your next summer social.

Makes 4 (2 units per glass)

1 lemon, quartered
1 lime, quartered
1 orange, quartered
2 tablespoons *Vodka Simple Syrup* (see page 129)
100ml (3½fl oz) *Orange Peel Vodka* (see page 142)
450ml (½ pint) dry white wine, chilled
300ml (10fl oz) sparkling mineral water or club soda, chilled
Additional lemon, lime and/or orange slices, to decorate

1 Put the fruit into a medium jug – squeezing each quarter as you go.
2 Add the remaining ingredients, stir well and serve in tall glasses filled with ice and decorated with fruit slices.

SPIRITED HOT CHOCOLATE

This ain't no kiddie cocoa.

Makes 2 (2.5 units per mug)

125ml (4fl oz) milk
225ml (8fl oz) milk chocolate, minimum 35 per cent cocoa solids, cut into very small pieces
110g (4oz) sugar
225ml (8fl oz) double cream
125ml (4fl oz) *Orange Peel Vodka* (see page 142) or vodka
½ teaspoon *Vanilla Vodka* (see page 143), or vanilla extract
Dash of chilli powder
Dash of salt
Vodka Whipped Cream (see page 119) or vanilla ice cream to serve (optional)

1 Heat the milk, chocolate and sugar in a medium saucepan placed over a pan of simmering water and whisk into a smooth mixture. Do not boil.
2 Whisk in the cream, both vodkas, chilli powder and salt.
3 Remove from the heat and serve in mugs topped with *Vodka Whipped Cream* or vanilla ice cream, if desired.

Instead of ice cream or whipped cream, my favourite way to serve Spirited Hot Cocoa is with a few marshmallows. The cocoa will slowly melt them into a gooey topping.

ESPRESSOTINI

This one will wake you up and give you a hug.

Makes 2 (2.3 units per glass)

225ml (8fl oz) freshly brewed espresso cooled to room temperature
75ml (3fl oz) vodka
40ml (1½fl oz) *Espresso Vodka* (see page 145) or coffee brandy
2 lemon twists (thin slices of lemon peel, pinched and twisted in the centre), to decorate

1 In a shaker, blend the espresso, the vodka and *Espresso Vodka* with ice by shaking vigorously for about 15 seconds
2 Strain into 2 large chilled martini glasses or snifters. Run a lemon twist around each rim and add to each glass.

HOT WHITE RUSSIAN

On a cold winter night, what could be better than to snuggle up to a hot white Russian?

Makes 4 (3 units per mug)
225ml (8fl oz) freshly brewed espresso
225ml (8fl oz) milk
225ml (8fl oz) double cream
175ml (6fl oz) vodka
125ml (4fl oz) *Espresso Vodka* (see page 145)
125ml (4fl oz) *Vodka Whipped Cream* (see page 119)

1 Stir together the first 5 ingredients in a saucepan over a moderate heat for about 5 minutes.
2 Pour into large mugs and top with *Vodka Whipped Cream*.

CUBAN MISSILE CRISIS

I discovered the mojito in Spain. If it didn't instantly become my favourite cocktail, it certainly gained that distinction after the week I spent in Cuba. And I had to find a way to sneak my variant into this book. So here is how Moscow meets Havana in a tall glass. It's a cold war cocktail.

Makes 2 (2 units per glass)

2 limes

3 tablespoons sugar

Crushed ice – enough to fill 2 glasses

Handful of fresh mint – leaves and stems

50ml (2fl oz) vodka

50ml (2fl oz) white rum (Havana Club,
    if available)

175–225ml (6–8fl oz) seltzer or soda water

1 Finely grate the lime zest and mix with 1 tablespoon of sugar with the zest from the limes on a small plate.

2 Cut the limes into quarters and moisten the rim of each glass with a lime quarter and coat the rims by turning them in the sugar mixture. Fill each glass with ice.

3 In a shaker, add the remaining sugar and the mint (reserve 2 sprigs for garnish).

4 Add the limes (reserving 2 quarters for garnish) to the shaker, squeezing the juice from each wedge as you drop them in.

5 With a long wooden spoon, mash and muddle the limes with the sugar and mint.

6 Add the vodka and rum and shake several times. Strain the mixture into glasses.

7 Fill each glass to the top with seltzer and garnish with a mint sprig and lime wedge.

You can substitute a lemon/lime soda for the soda water and reduce the amount of sugar.

APPLE VODKA COCKTAIL

Here's what really happens when apples get sauced.

Makes 2 (1.5 units per glass)
75ml (3fl oz) *Apple Vodka* (see page 143)
2 teaspoons grenadine
2 teaspoons fresh lemon juice
2 apple slices, to garnish

1 Combine all the ingredients, shake with ice and strain into chilled cocktail glasses. Garnish with apple slices.

CHAMPAGNSKY KOKTAIL

A Mimosa with an attitudesky.

Makes 2 (1.5 units per glass)
125ml (4fl oz) champagne or sparkling white wine
40ml (1½fl oz) *Orange Peel Vodka* (see page 142)
50ml (2fl oz) freshly squeezed orange juice
Orange slices, to decorate

1 Pour all the ingredients – in the order given – into chilled champagne glasses and decorate with orange slices.

MOLOTOV COCKTAIL

Like its namesake, this Molotov Cocktail burns all the way to its target – which in this case is your stomach. But it hurts so good.

Makes 4 (1.6 units per glass)
125ml (4fl oz) Sour Cherry Vodka (see page 146)
30ml (1fl oz) Chilli Vodka (see page 145)

1 Blend the vodkas in a shaker with ice by shaking vigorously for about 15 seconds.
2 Strain into chilled shot glasses.

Care to play a cocktail version of Russian roulette? Make one shot extra spicy. You can figure out the rest.

The real Molotov Cocktail, *Molotov* ('the hammer'), was the pseudonym of Viacheslav Skriabin, Stalin's Commissar for Foreign Affairs, who signed a pact with Nazi Germany in 1939 which effectively blocked Finland from acquiring weapons to defend itself against the Red Army aggression. The lack of adequate anti-tank weapons forced the soldiers to destroy the Soviet tanks through close-in fighting, using improvised devices. One such device (consisting of a bottle filled with a mixture of petrol, sand and soap suds, with a burning rag in its mouth) was named after the man and the pact that the Finnish soldiers blamed for their plight; and the 'Molotov Cocktail' was born.

TO HONEY

ACKNOWLEDGEMENTS

I would like to thank my Mom, 'Honey', for talking me through the first meals I ever ruined. I miss her.

Special thanks to my Dad who, by example, demonstrated to me at a young age that cooking wasn't 'just for girls' at a time when few men in America could even find the kitchen. I also want to thank my brother, Christopher Rose for his inspiration and support (plus I know how much he loves to see his name in print). Big hugs to my aunt Kay Puleio for many enthusiastic cooking discussions and to my cousins Cathy and Bob Sylvia for their gift of an electric mixer, without which I might still be on page 119.

Thank you Muna Reyal, the best cookbook editor I ever had (in fact, the only cookbook editor I ever had, but terrific nonetheless), the inimitable Kyle Cathie and everyone at Kyle Cathie Ltd. A round of applause, please, for Carl Hodson, Simon Wheeler and Annie Rigg for making these recipes look so much better than they really are.

And cheers to my friends John McCrae and Michael Albano. In their own way, they each inspired me to be a better cook. John exposed me to professional technique; Michael shared his love affair with comfort foods. Add to the list Janie Mann (so she'll stop saying I never thank her for anything) and Jennifer Templeton (because she told me to) and my cousin Frank Puleio (who makes a mean martini). Let's not forget Giovanni Contrada. But then again, who could? And for a good time call Terri Davis. Or Tacia Terzis. And if Jon Stetson is such a great magician, why couldn't he make disco disappear? But that's just the vodka talking.

My appreciation extends to my son, John, who is now – and I somehow suspect shall forever remain – my toughest food critic. There's just no misunderstanding the word 'yuck!'

And, most important, my undying gratitude goes to my better half, Galina, who chopped, diced, sliced, scrubbed and encouraged me throughout the preparation of this book. I couldn't have done it without her – though I'm certain she wishes I had. I have no idea why or how she's put up with me all these years. I'm not that good a cook.

Photo by Galina Savina

When John Rose isn't writing about food and travel, he is the award-winning creative director of Rose Creative Strategies in Moscow, where he has produced thousands of ads and commercials for many of the world's best-known brands.

DRINKAWARE.CO.UK

First published in Great Britain in 2005 by
Kyle Cathie Limited
122 Arlington Road, London NW1 7HP
general.enquiries@kyle-cathie.com
www.kylecathie.com

10 9 8 7 6 5 4 3 2 1

ISBN 1 85626 639 7

Text © 2005 John Rose
Photography © 2005 Simon Wheeler, except for p84–85 © Alamy, p130–131 © Renzo Mazzolini/The Smirnoff Co., p156–157 © The Smirnoff Co.
Book design © 2005 Kyle Cathie Limited

Senior editor: Muna Reyal
Designer: Carl Hodson
Photographer: Simon Wheeler
Food stylist: Annie Rigg
Props stylist: Roisin Nield
Copy editor: Stephanie Horner
Editorial assistant: Cecilia Desmond
Production: Sha Huxtable and Alice Holloway

A Cataloguing In Publication record for this title is available from the British Library.

Colour reproduction by Chromagraphic

Printed and bound in Singapore by Star Standard